Bloomsbury CPD Library: Marking and Feedback

By Sarah Findlater

BLOOMSBURY

LONDON · OXFORD · NEW YORK · NEW DELHI · SYDNEY

Bloomsbury Education
An imprint of Bloomsbury Publishing Plc

50 Bedford Square	1385 Broadway
London	New York
WC1B 3DP	NY 10018
UK	USA

www.bloomsbury.com

Bloomsbury is a registered trade mark of Bloomsbury Publishing Plc

First published 2016

© Sarah Findlater, 2016

British Library Cataloguing-in-Publication Data
A catalogue record for this book is available from the British Library.

ISBN:
PB 9781472918161
ePub 9781472918185
ePDF 9781472918178

Library of Congress Cataloguing-in-Publication Data
A catalogue record for this book is available from the Library of Congress.

10 9 8 7 6 5 4 3 2 1

Typeset by Integra Software Services Pvt. Ltd.
Printed by CPI Group (UK) Ltd, Croydon, CR0 4YY

This book is produced using paper that is made from wood grown in managed, sustainable forests. It is natural, renewable and recyclable. The logging and manufacturing processes conform to the environmental regulations of the country of origin.

To view more of our titles please visit www.bloomsbury.com

Contents

I would like to dedicate this book to the headteachers that I have worked with. It is a tough job at the top. You have all been so very different in your approaches to steering the ship and I have learned a great deal from each of you.

How to use this book

The Bloomsbury CPD Library provides primary and secondary teachers with affordable, comprehensive and accessible 'do-it-yourself' continuing professional development. This book focuses on the important skill of providing all students with useful and efficient marking and feedback to help them progress and reach their full potential.

The book is split into two halves: Part 1 **Teach yourself** and Part 2 **Train others**.

Teach yourself

This part of the book includes everything you need to improve your marking and feedback practice. It is split into four key stages:

STAGE 1: ASSESS

As well as providing an introduction to the main areas of marking and feedback, stage 1 includes a self-assessment questionnaire so that you can start the process of improving your practice with reflecting on what you already know and identifying the areas that you need to improve.

STAGE 2: IMPROVE

Stage 2 includes information about the different types of marking and feedback, the key theorists and what they say and how to put it into practice in the classroom. It introduces the marking and feedback cycle – a unique approach to improving your marking and feedback practice in the classroom.

STAGE 3: EVALUATE

Stage 3 offers a chance to evaluate how much you have improved so far and reflect on which areas still need improvement.

STAGE 4: EXCEL

This final stage looks ahead to how you can continue to improve and embed your good practice in the classroom as well as the rest of the school.

This comprehensive self-teach guide also includes teaching tips, to do lists at the end of each chapter and recommendations for how you can share your ideas and practice with other teachers in your school and beyond. A further reading recommendation or title to discuss in a CPD reading group is also included as well as a useful blog post to read in Blogger's corner.

By the end of part 1 you will have assessed, improved and consolidated your own marking and feedback practice.

Train others

Now that you are an expert in marking and feedback it's time to train others in your school! External training can be expensive and in-house training is hugely valuable as it can be made relevant to your training context – the teachers and children in your school. Whether it is one training session or a term's worth of training sessions there is advice and training plans in this section to help you get started, plan and implement marking and feedback training in your school. This section includes:

- Advice for running good CPD.
- A full set of training plans for running 1 extended twilight session, a series of 6 training sessions, or an Action research training programme.
- A full set of training PowerPoints which can be downloaded from the online resources that accompany this book.

See page 168 for an overview of the training plans.

Good luck with teaching yourself and training others! Keep us updated on your progress by tweeting using #BloomsCPD.

Online resources

For templates, questionnaires and Powerpoints from the book please visit www.bloomsbury.com/CPD-library-marking-feedback.

Part 1

Teach yourself

1

What's it all about?

Marking and feedback is a major part of every teacher's job regardless of your age, the subject you teach and the ability and age range of the students you teach. And if it isn't then it should be! The importance of good quality marking and feedback has been evidenced by many an academic study, and the benefits of a rigorous and refined approach to marking and feedback have been seen many a time in everyday classrooms where students are thriving and attainment levels are improving as a result.

Both the individual teacher's and the whole school's approach to marking and feedback needs to be well-thought-out, of high quality and appropriate for the individual school and classroom setting. The key is finding ways to make it powerful while also being manageable for all involved. Every teacher has struggled with their marking load and approach at some point in their career – this is normal.

Great marking builds great relationships

Providing good marking and feedback for your students is a vital way of communicating your thoughts and views on their work directly to them, and is a real bonding exercise for both sides. The value is clear when it is working two ways:

- care and appreciation is apparent from the teacher
- the student gives the marking time and feedback.

This is not something that will happen organically however. With each marking and feedback batch students receive, their understanding of your expectations of them will increase but you'll also need to train them on how to 'decode' your feedback and utilise your advice to improve. Giving students space to respond and interact in some way with the marking and feedback you have provided strengthens your bond, increases the impact of your feedback and builds the foundations for very effective marking and feedback practice. This is what you're aiming for. It takes time, planning and hard work but the pay-off is invaluable.

Marking highlights: the journey

Looking back over the work your students have produced and the progress they have made as a result of the marking and feedback will show you, the student and anyone else who cares to look (other members of staff, parents, Ofsted) the clear journey that the student has been on during their time with you. You should only expect the very best from each student at all times and this should be apparent in your marking and feedback. If they do not expect the very best of themselves, they soon will if you persevere. It is important that you make sure you train students to organise their work, be it in books, folders or online, in a manner that shows them and you how they have moved on. It is not just an exercise in making work look pretty, it really does help students appreciate their journey and is an honest reflection of their achievements.

Marking is planning

Marking and feedback are not only beneficial for the student in terms of knowing how they have done and what to do next to improve, they are also hugely beneficial for you. Marking is planning. Marking a set of books gives you a clear and realistic overview of how well the students have taken in the content of the lesson that was taught. It is easy to presume that because a certain topic or skill has been covered in a lesson students have learnt what they need to know, but a successful marking and feedback session might show that there are some students who need more support as well as some who need more stretch and challenge. This should directly influence how you approach your next lesson, or set of lessons, with those students before the marking session takes place.

Marking gives our students a real audience

When marking and feedback is a regular routine in the classroom, it is always apparent; work is of a higher quality, students take more time over their work, work is better organised, students are able to talk about their learning and results are improved. The students know they are writing for an audience and that the work will be seen and appreciated by you in the not too distant future. Having a real audience, albeit of one person, makes a real difference to the work produced by the student as it is not for their eyes only. Knowing that someone else will read it and have to understand the work as they do in their heads, changes how a student approaches that piece of work.

Marking enables progress

Having a well thought out and structured way of marking and feeding back to your students that both you and they are aware of, allows progress to flow and build rapidly. Within that structure, careful consideration needs to be given to the type of marking and feedback you are providing for your students. All subjects will have different demands and needs in terms of marking and

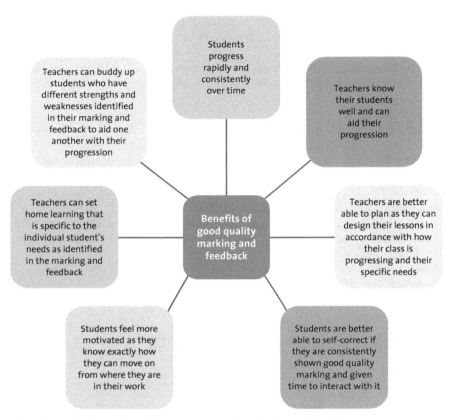

Fig. 1 Benefits of good quality marking and feedback – spider diagram

feedback, and a generic approach across all subjects or with students of all ages is never going to work. However, a common language and set routines can be established across subjects that allow the individual student to access marking and feedback in any subject with speed and ease. This will look different for individual schools. The right balance of praise and challenge is essential in order to provide encouragement while at the same time keeping the students focused on moving forward rather than just being 'happy' with their work. High expectations which are over and above their expected level of progress, is a powerful tool with all students. Marking and feedback can spur a student on to keep reaching higher goals, confident with the firm foundations both you and they have built through quality marking, feedback and student action.

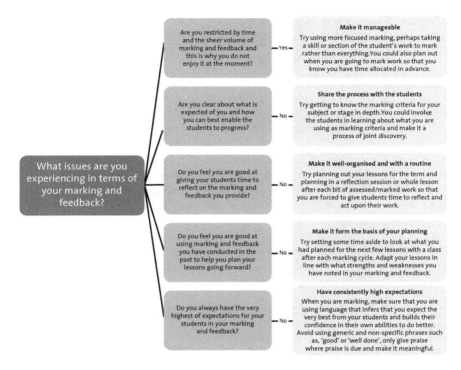

Fig. 2 What marking and feedback action might be best for you right now?

Marking vs feedback

Marking and feedback are inextricably interlinked and should be so, in order to have true impact upon your students. They can be pulled apart and defined, but are often more useful when used and looked at together.

Marking

Marking is considered to be more summative, demonstrating the extent to which the learner has met the success criteria set out and, often, how that contributes to the final grade or mark. It is used to measure learning and compare students against a standard or benchmark. It is usually used towards the end of a unit of teaching. It often directs thinking and solves problems. It generally quantifies achievement and acts as assessment of the learning achieved. The term 'marking' can also be used to refer to the simple annotation of right and wrong in a student's; work for instance with spelling, punctuation or calculations. It can also act as a simple indication that their work has been looked at by you.

Feedback

Feedback is formative and used to highlight the strengths and weaknesses in a piece of work produced with the aim of improvement going forward. Feedback gives the student detailed information to digest in relation to the work they have produced, and usually makes them think and act in response. Feedback can take the form of dialogue – either verbally or in written form – between student and teacher. Feedback acts as assessment for learning with the aim of moving the learning forward. It often provokes thinking and suggests next steps.

Below is a list of example effective/excellent and ineffective features of marking and feedback. These lists are by no mean inclusive of all elements of marking but do include some key ideas to think about.

Features of excellent marking and feedback:	Features of ineffective marking and feedback:
• Manageable	• Overambitious
• Has time allocated for students to reflect and act upon marking and feedback	• Inadequate time given for reflection and acting upon marking and feedback
• Well-organised and follows a routine	• Disorganised, erratic and no routine followed
• Forms the basis of your planning	• Does not inform planning
• A shared process with the students	• Students are unaware of the marking process
• Consistent high expectations	• Expectations are unclear from marking and feedback
• Common language across subjects	• Inaccessible language used
• Outcomes show clear impact	• Outcomes show lack of impact

Fig. 3 Features of excellent and ineffective marking and feedback

Chapter 1 takeaway

Teaching tip

Focus your marking and feedback

Whenever you are marking and giving feedback to your students consider these questions:

- Why am I saying this?
- What do I want them to do?
- Will it have impact if they do it?

This will really focus your marking and make sure that you are getting the most from your students when they revisit the work when you hand it back to them. You could for example focus on: a particular assessment objective in your subject area and key stage; a grammatical focus such as sentence variety or vocabulary; persuasive techniques and style or including key vocabulary for the relevant subject area accurately.

Pass it on

Sharing your ideas – within your school

Finding ways to share good practice in marking and feedback around your own school is so important. Don't just leave it to the person leading teaching and learning in your school, they cannot possibly know everything that goes on in every classroom. Sometimes just standing up and sharing your experiences is all that is needed to get things moving in your school and make immediate improvements; so be brave. Sharing what you do with marking and feedback will encourage others to do the same and start a really healthy academic conversation across the school. We can all learn from one another. You could, for example:

- share your experiences in whole-school meetings or CPD sessions
- email around some ideas and experiences and encourage others to do the same
- invite staff that are interested in marking and feedback to come along and share their ideas over lunch in your classroom
- start up a book club and read studies, websites and books that cover marking and feedback and discuss them monthly.

However you do it, just do it and get people talking and caring about what they do with marking and feedback in your school. The students will benefit and therefore so will you.

Colleague catch-up

Have a conversation with a colleague about what they consider the point of marking to be. Talk to them about your ideas and listen to their views. Speak to teachers in different subjects or key stages for interest. What are the differences and similarities with your viewpoints?

Share and tweet

Share your views on what you consider to be the point of marking and feedback on Twitter using the hashtag #BloomsCPD.

CPD book club recommendation

Dylan Wiliam and Paul Black, *Inside the Black Box*
(see Bibliography and further reading, page 295)

Bloggers' corner

Tom Sherrington has some great posts on marking and feedback that are well worth a read. Visit his blog at: headguruteacher.com

---

TO DO LIST:

- ☐ Reflect on what you consider the point of marking and feedback to be
- ☐ Reflect on your own marking and feedback routines and practices
- ☐ Tweet the conclusion of your reflections on the point of marking and feedback and check out what others have said by using the hashtag #BloomsCPD
- ☐ Speak to your colleagues about what they consider the point of marking and feedback to be
- ☐ Check out Tom Sherrington's blog posts on marking
- ☐ Read *Inside the Black Box* by Dylan Wiliam and Paul Black

2 Self-assessment

Being honest with yourself about how well you are performing in any particular area of your work is easier said than done. Often when looking at yourself it is hard to see things objectively. I find that it helps to think of the process of self-assessment as a safe place where you can be your most honest and open as no one else will be judging you but you.

How to complete the self-assessment questionnaire

On pages 16–33 there is a self-assessment questionnaire to encourage you to start the 'teach yourself' process by thinking very carefully about your current marking and feedback practice before you jump into trying to improve it.

When you are looking at your own marking and feedback practices and trying to form a clear view of where you are now and what the next steps will be, there are many ways of approaching it – it will depend on you as a person. For some people, it is useful to go with your gut and listen to the first thing that comes into your mind – your instinctual answer. For others, it is a better approach to spend a good amount of time really mulling over the self-assessment questions slowly and in detail.

Quick response approach

If your preference for the self-assessment is to go with your gut only, then simply fill in the quick response section after each question with the first thing that comes into your mind when you ask yourself the question. Do not mull over the question too long, simply read carefully and answer quickly. This approach will give you an overview of your current understanding and practice in marking and feedback and will take relatively little time. Just make sure you are uninterrupted, in a quiet place and able to complete the questionnaire in one sitting with no distractions so that you get focused and honest answers.

Considered response approach

If you choose to take a more reflective and detailed approach, then you can leave the quick response section blank and go straight onto reading the further guidance section under each question. This guidance provides prompt questions and ideas to get you thinking in detail about the question being asked and is designed to open up a wider scope in your answer. It will also enable you to look at your experience and pull examples into your answer to back up your statements. You may want to complete it a few questions at a time and take breaks, or you may be prepared to simply sit and work through the questions all in one sitting to ensure you remain focused. This approach does take longer, but it can lead to a more in-depth understanding of your current marking and feedback practice, and you will gain much more from the process than the quick response alone.

Combined approach

A thorough approach, and one I recommend, would be to use both approaches together regardless of personal preference. There is clear value in both approaches being used together. This would involve you firstly answering the self-assessment quick response questions by briefly noting down your instinctual answers for all questions. The next step would be to return to the start of the self-assessment, read the further guidance and then answer the questions once more, slowly and in detail forming more of a narrative around each question and pulling in examples from your own experience. Following this you would need to read over both responses and form a comprehensive and honest summary in your mind of your answers and a final view of where you feel you stand right now in your marking and feedback practice.

This is the longest of the three approaches to this questionnaire but will give you a comprehensive and full understanding of your current practice, thoughts and feelings in relation to marking and feedback. You will be surprised at the difference you see between the quick response and the considered response answers to the same questions. It can be very illuminating.

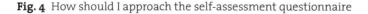

	Quick
• I have done this self-assessment before. • I only want a surface level overview of my current understanding and practice. • I work better when I work at speed. • I don't have much time.	Quick

	Considered
• I have never done this self-assessment before. • I want a deeper understanding of my current understanding and practice. • I work better when I take my time and really think things over. • I have some time to do this self-assessment.	Considered

	Combined
• I have never done this self-assessment before. • I have done this self-assessment before. • I want a comprehensive and full understanding of my current understanding and practice and want to compare that to what I thought before taking the self-assessment. • I have a decent amount of time to dedicate to completing this self-assessment.	Combined

Fig. 4 How should I approach the self-assessment questionnaire

Rate yourself

The final part of the self-assessment is to rate yourself. This section will ask you to rate your confidence and happiness in each area that has been covered in the questionnaire, with a view to working on these areas for improvement throughout the course of the book. The table below shows how the scale works: the higher the number you allocate yourself, the better you feel you are performing in that area.

Rating	Definition
1	Not at all. I don't. None at all. Not happy. Not confident at all.
2	Rarely. Barely. Very little. Very unconfident.
3	Not often at all. Not much. Quite unconfident.
4	Not particularly. Not really. Not a lot. Mildly unconfident.
5	Neutral. Unsure. Don't know. Indifferent.
6	Sometimes. At times. Moderately. A little bit. Mildly confident.
7	Quite often. A fair bit. Some. A little confident.
8	Most of the time. More often than not. Quite a lot. Quite confident.
9	The majority of the time. A lot. Very confident.
10	Completely. Very much so. A huge amount. Extremely happy. Extremely confident.

Fig. 5 Rate yourself definitions

Top tip

Self-assessment is a vital skill for self-reflection and progression in your professional life. It is important that we are honest, kind and constructive when it comes to self-assessing. It can be easy to be too harsh on yourself when you self-assess and allow your insecurities to cloud your judgment. Being objective and honest about yourself and your practice is a hard thing to do and it takes practice. Before you begin self-assessing, it is important to carefully consider the criteria you are using to assess yourself and focus on that at first without thinking about yourself. Feeling comfortable with what you are assessing will lead to a more accurate assessment. If you jump in and self-assess too early, before you have considered the assessment criteria, you may well have a clouded judgment and be unable to learn as much from the process. Don't rush it – it is too important.

Marking and feedback self-assessment questionnaire

QUESTION 1: Do you enjoy marking and giving feedback?

Quick response:

_____

_____

_____

_____

Questions for consideration

- What do you like about marking work or giving feedback to students?
- Do you enjoy reading over your students' work?
- What types of marking and feedback do you particularly enjoy?
- Do you have any routines that help you enjoy the marking and feedback process, e.g. listening to music, having a favourite snack, using special pens...?

Considered response:

_____

_____

_____

_____

_____

_____

_____

_____

_____

_____

Rate yourself

QUESTION 1: How much do you enjoy marking and feedback?

1   2   3   4   5   6   7   8   9   10

QUESTION 2: Do you feel your marking and feedback has impact upon student attainment and achievement in your classroom?

Quick response:

_____

_____

_____

_____

Questions for consideration

- Do you ever see students acting on your marking and feedback? When?
- Do you ever see a direct impact on your students' work following your marking and feedback? When?
- Why do you think your marking had an impact on those occasions?
- What could you do to make more of an impact with your marking and feedback?
- What examples can you think of when you have seen students directly acting upon your marking and feedback?
- What examples can you think of when students have been able to move forward and show progression in their work as a result of your marking and feedback?

Considered response:

_____

_____

_____

_____

_____

_____

Rate yourself

QUESTION 2: How much impact on student achievement and attainment do you feel your marking and feedback has at the moment?

1   2   3   4   5   6   7   8   9   10

QUESTION 3: What is your general approach to marking and feedback?

Quick response:

_____

_____

_____

_____

Questions for consideration

- Do you always approach marking and feedback in the same manner or do you mix up your approaches?
- Are you organised and routined with your marking and feedback or erratic and disorganised?
- Do you make time in lessons to include marking students' work as they go?
- Do you mark some work every evening to keep on top of the load or do you take all books home every weekend and spend one session marking them all at once?
- Do you have a system you follow every week so all books are marked and up to date?
- Do you pride yourself in keeping on top of marking and feedback or do you often find yourself behind?

Considered response:

_____

_____

_____

_____

_____

_____

_____

Rate yourself

QUESTION 3: How happy are you with your approach to marking and feedback at the moment?

1	2	3	4	5	6	7	8	9	10

QUESTION 4: What educational research, theories or case studies on marking and feedback do you know about and how does this inform or influence your practice?

Quick response:

_____

_____

_____

_____

Questions for consideration

- Do you have any knowledge of the education research or case studies about marking and feedback? What do you know?
- Do you value educational research into marking and feedback?
- What has stopped you looking into research on marking and feedback, e.g. lack of time or desire or it has never crossed your mind?
- Do you feel it should be part of your job to look at educational research on marking and feedback or is it someone else's job?
- Have you discussed research or case studies on marking and feedback with any colleagues?
- Have you conducted any research into marking and feedback yourself or as part of a team with your school setting? If so, what was the process like and what were the outcomes?
- How do you feel teachers or schools as a whole should use the findings of educational research on marking and feedback?

Considered response:

_____

_____

_____

_____

_____

Rate yourself

QUESTION 4: How confident are you with your knowledge of educational research into marking and feedback?

| 1 | 2 | 3 | 4 | 5 | 6 | 7 | 8 | 9 | 10 |

QUESTION 5: Do you feel your views on marking and feedback match those of the school you work in?

Quick response:

_____

_____

_____

_____

Questions for consideration:

- Is your whole-school marking and feedback policy lengthy and detailed or short and concise?
- Is your whole-school marking and feedback policy highly prescriptive or more generalised?
- Is there anything that you feel is not right or does not work for you in your whole-school marking and feedback policy? If so, why?
- What do you like about your whole-school marking and feedback policy?
- How do you feel students and parents feel about the whole-school marking and feedback policy?
- If you could design the whole-school marking and feedback policy, what would it look like and why?

Considered response:

_____

_____

_____

_____

_____

_____

_____

Rate yourself

QUESTION 5: How closely do you feel you and your school's views on marking align?

1	2	3	4	5	6	7	8	9	10

QUESTION 6: Do you feel your views on marking and feedback match those of the department you work in?

Quick response:

_____

_____

_____

_____

Questions for consideration

- Do you feel that your department's approach to marking and feedback are in line with what you consider important for the subject or age range you teach?
- What do you feel your department does well and not so well in terms of marking and feedback?
- Are there any pressure points in the year for your department and if so, does your department's approach to marking and feedback take this into account?
- If you had full power over your department's marking and feedback approach with no outside influence, what would it look like?

Considered response:

_____

_____

_____

_____

_____

_____

_____

_____

_____

_____

Rate yourself

QUESTION 6: How closely do you feel yours and your department's views on marking align?

1	2	3	4	5	6	7	8	9	10

QUESTION 7: Where do you feel your strengths lie in marking and feedback?

Quick response:

_____

_____

_____

_____

Questions for consideration

- What do you feel you do well in your marking and feedback?
- Have you developed these strengths over time or have you always been good in these areas of marking and feedback?
- Do you have any strengths in marking and feedback that you used to have that are now not quite as strong – if so why?
- Are there any elements of your marking and feedback that you have been praised for either by in-school monitoring, colleagues, students or parents?

Considered response:

_____

_____

_____

_____

_____

_____

_____

_____

_____

_____

_____

Rate yourself

QUESTION 7: How confident do you feel when it comes to your marking and feedback practice?

| 1 | 2 | 3 | 4 | 5 | 6 | 7 | 8 | 9 | 10 |

QUESTION 8: Where do you feel your weaknesses lie in marking and feedback?

Quick response:

_____
_____
_____
_____

Questions for consideration

- What do you feel you are not particularly good at with your marking and feedback?
- Have you always been weak in this area of marking and feedback or have you worsened in this area over time?
- Do you have any weaknesses in marking and feedback that you used to have that are now much improved – if so why?
- Are there any weak elements of your marking and feedback that have been mentioned or highlighted to you either by in-school monitoring, colleagues, students or parents?
- Have you been offered any help or training for these weaknesses in marking and feedback?
- Have you undertaken any training or reading in your weak marking and feedback areas in your own time?

Considered response:

_____
_____
_____
_____
_____
_____

Rate yourself

QUESTION 8: How serious do you feel your weaknesses are when it comes to marking and feedback?

1	2	3	4	5	6	7	8	9	10

QUESTION 9: What would you like to try in your marking and feedback practices that you have not already tried?

Quick response:

_____

_____

_____

_____

Questions for consideration

- Have you spotted a gap in your marking and feedback practices that you feel needs filling? What approaches have you considered to fill this gap?
- Is there an approach to marking and feedback that you have read about or seen used in another classroom by a colleague that you have not yet tried in your own classroom?
- What has stopped you trying it so far?

Considered response:

_____

_____

_____

_____

_____

_____

_____

_____

_____

_____

_____

Rate yourself

QUESTION 9: How confident do you feel about trying something new with marking and feedback?

1	2	3	4	5	6	7	8	9	10

QUESTION 10: Is there anything that is holding you back in developing your marking and feedback?

Quick response:

_____

_____

_____

_____

Questions for consideration

- What do you dread about marking and feedback?
- What are you not particularly good at when it comes to marking and feedback?
- What have you tried to overcome time and time again in your marking and feedback but failed to move forward from?
- What training do you feel you are lacking in your marking and feedback?
- What constraints do you feel you have placed upon you when it comes to your marking and feedback?
- What have you done to overcome these hurdles in you marking and feedback?

Considered response:

_____

_____

_____

_____

_____

_____

_____

_____

_____

Rate yourself

QUESTION 10: How much are these things holding you back in terms of improving your marking and feedback?

1	2	3	4	5	6	7	8	9	10

QUESTION 11: Is there any aspect of marking and feedback that you have seen work for others but has not worked for you?

Quick response:

_____

_____

_____

_____

Questions for consideration

- Have you tried an approach to marking and feedback that a colleague swears by, a book raves about or a blog has recommended that has just not worked for you?
- What did it involve?
- What hurdles did you face?
- Why did it ultimately not work for you?
- Do you know of others it has worked for?
- What is different for them, e.g. personality, time, subject, age or school setting?
- Would you try it again?

Considered response:

_____

_____

_____

_____

_____

_____

_____

_____

Rate yourself

QUESTION 11: How confident do you feel with your own marking and feedback when you consider others teachers' practices?

| 1 | 2 | 3 | 4 | 5 | 6 | 7 | 8 | 9 | 10 |

QUESTION 12: What do your students think of your marking?

Quick response:

_____

_____

_____

_____

Questions for consideration

- Have you ever spoken to your students about your marking and feedback in a lesson?
- What was their response?
- Did they need lots of clarification about your approach or did they understand it easily?
- Have you conducted any interviews or questionnaires about your marking and feedback with students? If so, what were your findings?
- Have you ever adapted anything in response to students' comments about your marking and feedback?

Considered response:

_____

_____

_____

_____

_____

_____

_____

_____

Rate yourself

QUESTION 12: How confident are you that you really know what students feel and think about your marking and feedback?

1   2   3   4   5   6   7   8   9   10

QUESTION 13: What do you think students like when it comes to marking and feedback?

Quick response:

_____

_____

_____

_____

Questions for consideration

- What do you find your students really seem to like when it comes to marking and feedback, e.g. getting a sticker or stamp in their book, being allocated a grade, receiving a personal comment, you marking in a certain colour of pen...?
- Do they relish a clear and concise target with specific actions to undertake?
- Do they like regular marking and feedback lessons to take in your comments and act upon them?
- Do they like lots of ticks and annotations on the page or prefer just comments at the end?
- Do they like self and/or peer marking in class or prefer your marking and feedback?

Considered response:

_____

_____

_____

_____

_____

_____

_____

_____

Rate yourself

QUESTION 13: How certain are you about knowing what students like when it comes to marking and feedback?

1   2   3   4   5   6   7   8   9   10

QUESTION 14: What do you feel students need when it comes to marking and feedback?

Quick response:

_____

_____

_____

_____

Questions for consideration

- Put aside what the students may like – what do you think they actually need when it comes to marking and feedback?
- What marking and feedback have you seen have an impact on students' work?
- Of the aspects of marking and feedback that your students seem to like, which seem to have a positive impact on their work?

Considered response:

_____

_____

_____

_____

_____

_____

_____

_____

_____

_____

Rate yourself

QUESTION 14: How confident are you that you know what students need when it comes to marking and feedback?

1	2	3	4	5	6	7	8	9	10

QUESTION 15: DO you know what parents and carers think of your marking?

Quick response:

_____

_____

_____

_____

Questions for consideration

- Have you ever spoken to the parents or carers of your students about your marking and feedback, for instance at parents evening or over the phone?
- What was their response?
- Did they need lots of clarification on your approach or did they understand it easily?
- Have you conducted any interviews or questionnaires about your marking and feedback with parents and carers? If so, what were your findings?
- Have you ever adapted anything in response to parents' and carers' comments about marking and feedback?

Considered response:

_____

_____

_____

_____

_____

_____

_____

_____

Rate yourself

QUESTION 15: How confident are you that you know what parents think about your marking and feedback of their child's work?

1	2	3	4	5	6	7	8	9	10

QUESTION 16: What do you feel parents and carers like when it comes to marking and feedback?

Quick response:

_____

_____

_____

_____

Questions for consideration

- What are the most common compliments parents give to marking and feedback they see in books?
- Do they react better to any particular techniques, e.g. use of stickers/stamps, marking in certain colours, inclusion of grades, personal comments, allocation of targets and specific actions?
- Do they like lots of marking and feedback on their child's work or prefer less on the page for their child to take in at any one time?
- Do they like regular marking and feedback lessons to allow their child to take in your comments and act upon them?
- Do they like lots of ticks and annotations on the page or prefer just comments at the end?
- Do they like self and/or peer marking in class or prefer your marking and feedback?

Considered response:

_____

_____

_____

_____

_____

Rate yourself

QUESTION 16: How confident are you that you know what your students' parents and carers like when it comes to marking and feedback?

1	2	3	4	5	6	7	8	9	10

QUESTION 17: What do you feel parents and carers need when it comes to marking and feedback?

Quick response:

_____

_____

_____

_____

Questions for consideration

- Put aside what you think the parents and carers like – what do they actually need when it comes to marking and feedback?
- What are they entitled to see in their child's book in order to understand how they are doing?
- Should parents and carers have a say in the marking and feedback that is carried out in your classroom?

Considered response:

_____

_____

_____

_____

_____

_____

_____

_____

_____

_____

Rate yourself

QUESTION 17: How confident are you that you know what your students' parents and carers actually need when it comes to marking and feedback?

| 1 | 2 | 3 | 4 | 5 | 6 | 7 | 8 | 9 | 10 |

QUESTION 18: Do you have an understanding of what other staff think of your marking?

Quick response:

_____

_____

_____

_____

Questions for consideration

- Have you ever spoken to colleagues about your marking and feedback, e.g. in department marking moderation or with a more senior member of staff following marking and feedback monitoring?
- What was their response?
- Did they need lots of clarification on your approach or did they understand it easily?
- Have you conducted any interviews or questionnaires about your marking and feedback with colleagues? If so, what were your findings?
- Have you ever adapted anything in response to a colleague's comments about marking and feedback?

Considered response:

_____

_____

_____

_____

_____

_____

_____

_____

Rate yourself

QUESTION 18: How confident are you that you know what colleagues think about your marking and feedback?

1	2	3	4	5	6	7	8	9	10

The results

Well done, you have self-evaluated your practices in marking and feedback and are now a step forward in the right direction to becoming a master marker and giver of feedback. You have considered your personal approach; whether you enjoy it; whether you feel you have impact; how confident you are in terms of educational research; how well your views fit that of your school and department; your strengths and weaknesses; what you want to try; your student's, parent's, carer's and colleague's thoughts on your marking and feedback. It is a lot to take in so take the time to let your self-assessment sink in and sit with them for a while.

Take a look at how you rated your answers for each question in the questionnaire and compare your ratings with the chart below which will guide you to taking the next steps in your marking and feedback.

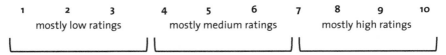

Fig. 6 How did you rate yourself?

Mostly low ratings

You have a way to go with your marking and feedback, but you are at the start of an exciting journey right now and the sky is the limit. You have a lot to learn but it will all have a positive impact on your students and improve your teaching at the same time. Everyone is a winner. Now is the time to pick your first area of development and really get your teeth into marking and feedback in your classroom. One step at a time, you will form a great marking and feedback routine that will make your job even more satisfying and enjoyable.

Mostly medium ratings

You have trialled a few marking and feedback practices in your time and you are most definitely not a novice in this area of teaching and learning. However, there is lots that you can still do to make sure that your marking and feedback has maximum impact every day with all of your students. You need to take the time to prioritise the areas of marking and feedback that you now want to become expert in to take you to the next level. The exciting thing is that you are not that far away from mastery. You just need to focus and hone your skills and knowledge to become great in this area of your profession.

Mostly high ratings

You are confident in your marking and feedback practices. You have done a lot of reading and research. There are areas that you could begin to train others in straight away; to help them master the things you have battled hard to perfect or at the very least make excellent. Identify the areas you can still improve in and make sure you do not get complacent about those areas you feel are already very strong. Always be on the lookout for new ideas that you can learn from others even if you are really confident in your marking and feedback knowledge and skills. We can often learn a huge amount by teaching others about something as it opens our eyes to new angles in the topic. Remember that we are learners and we can always get better.

Now what?

The results are in. So now what? You have a full and detailed self-reflection on your marking and feedback practices and it is important that you now make the most of it. Take the time to action plan as a result of the answers you have given and the conclusions you have drawn. Don't make this simply another bit of paperwork you have completed. Use it to really open your eyes to how far you have come, where you are now and what you want to do next. Prioritise what you want to work on and get going on it.

Chapter 2 takeaway

Teaching tip

Don't throw the baby out with the bath water

It is easy to be hard on yourself when you are self-assessing – we are our own worst critics. Yes it is important to know what you need to improve upon but don't forget all that you are wonderful at too! Think about your marking and feedback practice carefully and know what you do well. If there are things that you have seen have impact with your students then make sure you keep on doing them and share that practice with others.

Pass it on

Sharing your ideas – why it is good to share

Once you start reflecting, researching, discussing and trying out new marking and feedback techniques, theories and ideas it is only right that you share your newly acquired skills and knowledge with others. How you do that is a very individual choice, but there are many options out there.

Whether you prefer face-to-face conversations or written word, one-to-one or group sessions, strangers or familiar faces, there are options out there for you to share the great practice that you have been honing and perhaps learn from others too. Often the questions that others raise when you share good practice can help you to develop even further than you realised was possible. Opening yourself to the possibility of criticism is a scary prospect but it is so important to do so in order to better yourself.

Team discussion
Suggest using the questions from the questionnaire to form the basis of a discussion on marking and feedback with the rest of the team you work with in your next team meeting. You may be surprised at who has similar or very different answers and views to you.

Share and tweet
Share your views about what you have realised or found of interest while doing this questionnaire on Twitter using the hashtag #BloomsCPD.

CPD Book club recommendation
John Hattie, *Visible Learning for Teachers*
(See Bibliography and further reading, page 295)

Bloggers' corner
David Didau has some thought-provoking posts on marking and feedback that are well worth a read. Visit his blog at: http://www.learningspy.co.uk.

TO DO LIST:

☐ Leave a little time after completing the questionnaire and then re-read your answers and really reflect on what they reveal
☐ Consider any area that you would like to work on that have been highlighted by the questionnaire
☐ Tweet the conclusion of anything you have realised or found interesting while doing the questionnaire and check out what others have said by using the hashtag #BloomsCPD
☐ Discuss the questionnaire questions as a team next time you meet together
☐ Check out David Didau's blog posts on marking
☐ Read *Visible Learning for Teachers* by John Hattie

3

Types of marking and feedback

There are many approaches to marking and feedback in the classroom and they all have their benefits and disadvantages. It is important that whichever approach you choose to take is fit for purpose. As with many aspects of teaching, and indeed life, it is best to begin with the end-game in mind and work backwards.

- What do you want the student to come away with after looking at and interacting with your marking and feedback?

- What do you want them to do with that marking and feedback?

Once you have the answers to these questions clear in your mind, then a relevant approach should be easy to select. It is great to experiment with different types of marking but always let your students know why you are taking that approach and talk it through with them, so that they get the most out of it. Avoid confusion by discussing your approaches to marking and feedback with your students. Try not to make things more complex than necessary or overload students with too many approaches at close intervals. The more you educate and involve your students in the marking and feedback approaches you are using and their purpose, the more easily your students will be able to understand your marking and feedback and begin to be able to access it at a higher level.

Formative and summative

Marking and feedback strategies broadly fall into two categories: formative and summative.

Formative

Formative marking and feedback can take many forms, but however it is approached the core goal is to monitor student learning and progress and provide ongoing feedback that can lead to improvements in the students' work and the teacher's instruction. It should help students identify their strengths and weaknesses in their work and help teachers in their grouping of students in class to aid their progression. Good examples of formative marking and feedback provide exemplars and advice as to what the students' next step to improve is. It does not require gradings and can be applied to small or larger pieces of work with ease.

Summative

Summative marking and feedback can also take many forms, but however it is approached the core goal is to evaluate students' learning and progress. Summative marking often involves a grade and is usually used in exams and final unit texts to assess and feedback where that student is in line with a class, school or national benchmark. It is often used to quantify and reward achievement as well as produce data.

Marking and feedback approaches

I have outlined below a number of different approaches to marking and feedback that are commonplace in classrooms now or were in the past. Take some time to think about whether you use, or have in the past used, these marking approaches in your classroom and what your experience was with each. What do you find works best with students at particular ages or in certain subjects etc.?

Close

Overview:
Close marking and feedback is detailed and in-depth marking. It involves a thorough reading of the student's work with detailed and often extensive annotations about the content and whether assessment criteria are met or unmet.

Strengths:
Used sparingly and with a structured lesson guiding the student on how to interact with the marking and act upon it, it can be useful with some groups of students.

Weaknesses:
This type of marking and feedback looks impressive on the page but can often be overwhelming for students. Many students would not be able to retain the quantity of feedback that this type of marking provides and some will switch off because of the amount of reading and processing involved in going over the marking. Teachers can spend an unreasonable, and quite frankly an unmanageable, amount of time marking books if this is the approach they take for every piece of work produced – and some teachers do this!

When you might use it:
When marking and giving feedback on important pieces of work, such as exam coursework. Students needs to be given time and space immediately after receiving this marked work and taught how to act upon the feedback. They will need to be very familiar with the mark scheme or rubric you are using with them in order for this to work well.

Student input:
You can really get students to engage well with this type of marking and feedback if you give them adequate training and ample time to work through your annotations.

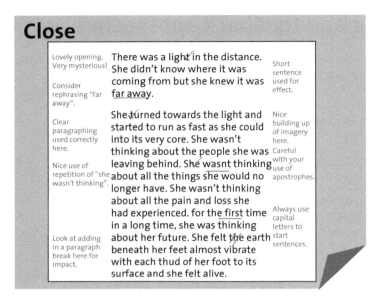

Fig. 7 Examples of marking – Close

Focused

Overview:

Focused marking and feedback allows the teachers, and indeed the students receiving the feedback, to focus on one specific element of their work. For instance, you may focus on the use of punctuation, subject-specific vocabulary or expression in a particular piece of work. The focus is generally shared prior to the work being completed to allow the student to really focus on that element of their work while creating it, as well as when looking at how to improve it once feedback has been given.

Strengths:

This type of marking and feedback can really help develop a student in a specific area of concern and improve upon it quickly. The teacher needs to be mindful that other skills do not slip because of the focus – expectations need to remain high of the work as a whole but with the knowledge that feedback will be specific and focused on that element to aim rapid improvement. If this type of marking is used for lots of different subject-specific assessment focuses on rotation, it can really help students to become confident with what is actually expected of them. Teachers can also benefit, as marking is generally quicker with this approach.

Weaknesses:

Obviously, you are not marking everything the student has done so some errors will go unchecked in the student's view and could possibly be seen as correct

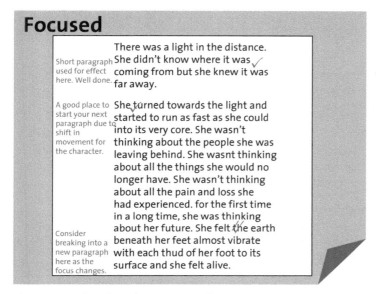

Fig. 8 Examples of marking – Focused

when they are not. The rationale behind this approach needs to be clearly explained to students so that they do not think the rest of the piece is perfect.

When you might use it:

When a particular skill is holding a student back from progressing then a clear and open focus on that skill alone will help them hone in on that skill and then apply it in other contexts.

Student input:

This type of marking allows students to really look deeply into an aspect of their work without being overwhelmed by the entire piece being marked. You can set them some really challenging tasks based on their learning from looking at the focused marking.

Selective

Overview:

Selective marking and feedback entails the teacher selecting a particular section of the work produced by the student and marking only that section. The marking can take the form of close or focused marking and feedback but will only be for the specific section of work. The teacher can choose to make the student aware in advance of the section that they will feedback on or they can keep them guessing and ensure that they do not lose focus in other sections of the work produced. It may, for example, be a paragraph picked at random, a chosen section of a write-up or essay or the beginning and end of the work only.

Strengths:

This allows the student to focus on the marking without being overloaded or seeing the same corrections over and over throughout their work. It also allows the marking to be more manageable for the teachers.

Weaknesses:

Again, you are not marking everything the student has done so some errors will go unchecked. Discussion of this approach is required before you present their work back to the students.

When you might use it:

This approach is useful if you want the student to really start to look in detail at the strengths and weaknesses of their work, but you also want them to be able to digest the feedback you are giving them.

Student input:

This type of marking allows students to fully focus on a smaller section of their work and hone their skills rather than having to take on the whole piece which some could find unmanageable.

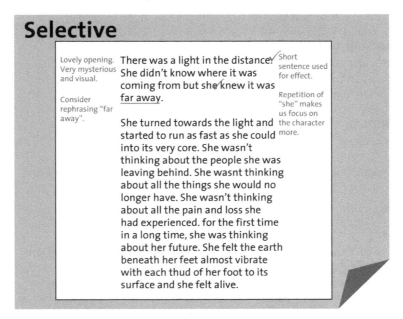

Fig. 9 Examples of marking – Selective

Incorrect red herring

Overview:

Incorrect feedback involves the teacher deliberately making one of the elements of their marking and feedback incorrect and challenging the student to decipher which element that might be. For instance, in the example below the teacher has incorrectly marked a spelling as incorrect but all other feedback is correct and useful. This can be differentiated and hints provided to aid discovery. This type of marking, as with most, is best followed immediately with an activity to ensure the student is showing progress on the element of marking that was incorrect in order to embed the feedback given and learning that has taken place. It is important that all students discover the correct red herring and then act upon that error so that further mistakes are not made.

Strengths:

The student is forced to engage with all the marking and feedback provided with a focus on the detail in order to try and work out which is incorrect. It gets them thinking.

Weaknesses:

If they are weak in a certain skill then they may not be able to spot the error.

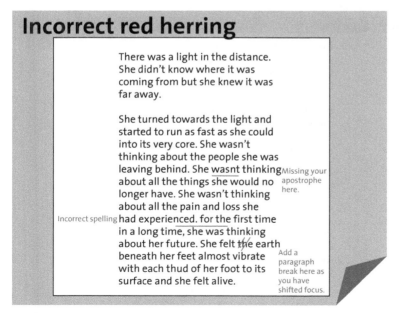

Fig. 10 Examples of marking – Incorrect red herring

When you might use it:

When you want to test a student who claims to be comfortable with a skill but where you have your doubts. Get testing them.

Student input:

Students really need to engage with your marking and feedback comments in this type of marking and feedback. They cannot just passively read your feedback, they need to actively engage with it and think about what each comment means in order to spot the red herring.

Coding

Overview:

Marking and feedback that uses codes requires the teacher to formulate a list of elements they mark or feed back on in students' work within their subject area, and assign a code to each element. All students are then provided with a list of these codes and their attached meaning. When the teacher marks work they only use codes and no actual written feedback. Usually when work is given back, the student must look up the code and write out the relevant meaning, e.g. P – punctuation error.

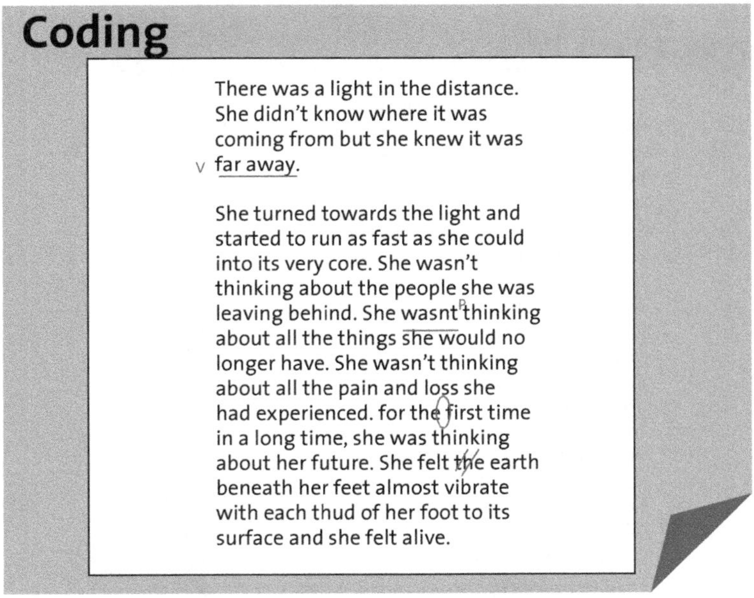

Coding

> There was a light in the distance. She didn't know where it was coming from but she knew it was
> v far away.
>
> She turned towards the light and started to run as fast as she could into its very core. She wasn't thinking about the people she was leaving behind. She wasnt thinking about all the things she would no longer have. She wasn't thinking about all the pain and loss she had experienced. for the first time in a long time, she was thinking about her future. She felt the earth beneath her feet almost vibrate with each thud of her foot to its surface and she felt alive.

Fig. 11 Examples of marking – Coding

Strengths:
Coding can be used for both positive and negative marking and feedback. It ensures that the student has read the feedback and can aid memory recall of aspects of their work that they need to build on. This approach can save the teacher time but will take up class time which will need planning into lessons.

Weaknesses:
This approach takes time as students will need to look up and write out the targets before responding to them. If you have students with special educational needs or of low ability just make sure that adequate time and differentiation is factored into your lesson plan when they are receiving the feedback.

When you might use it:
When you are marking for many different assessment focuses in one piece of work, this will save marking time. Also, if students have become lazy when they receive feedback then this can ensure they are working hard and connecting with the marking.

Student input:
Students need to actually write out the corresponding comments to go with your coding so this type of marking and feedback really does make students work for their feedback. They are forced to look at the success criteria and also select the correct focuses to write into their books.

Verbal

Overview:
Verbal marking and feedback involves the teacher circulating while the students are working and providing verbal feedback that is specific and useful that the students can act upon as they work. The best practice includes the student clearly noting down what has been said to them and immediately acting on that feedback in their work. This type of marking and feedback requires a routine in place where students are used to getting on independently in a quiet, focused manner, while the teacher circulates so that students are concentrating on their work and able to receive and act on the teacher's feedback without interruption.

Strengths:
This type of marking allows the teacher and student to have a dialogue about marking face to face which is powerful for students and can have more impact

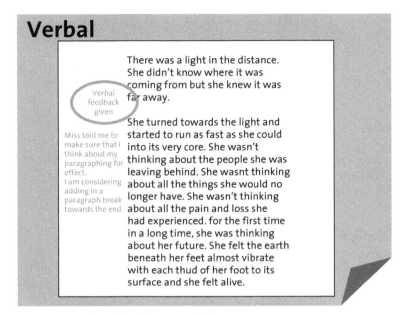

Fig. 12 Examples of marking – verbal

than written feedback if done well. It also allows the student to have ownership of the marking and feedback process as they can question it. It can also allow for live marking: marking during the lesson before they have completed the work, enabling them to take in corrections as they work.

Weaknesses:

It takes time for teachers to speak with students individually in a useful manner, so this will need to be well-planned and specific and focused on impact and improvement. Some students may respond better to written feedback where they can read and think about it independently.

When you might use it:

When you want students to consider their work as they write and improve as they go along rather than after they finish.

Student input:

Students have to write your verbal comments in their books as you are saying them, so they are forced to pay attention to your words. This can be powerful. You can also get them to write a commitment from them under your words addressing how they are going to do what you have asked them to do.

Electronic

Overview:

There are many great tools out there that allow for brilliant electronic marking and feedback and there will be many more going forward. Some great tools that have stood the test of time so far include: *Google Drive*, *Google Classroom*, *Edmodo* and *Turn It In*. There are many more, but exploring them all is for another book! These tools and platforms allow the teacher to feed back electronically, enabling a portfolio of work, feedback and progress to be easily accessible for individual students and saved for as long as necessary (e.g. an entire year or key stage) to look back over. Some of these tools allow live marking while the student is working. The teacher can access their work remotely from their own computer and provide feedback to the student as they are going along, and can witness students then immediately editing and improving their work. Some of the tools also allow parental access to enable parents to view a student's work and the teacher feedback. Parents can even partake in the process, if appropriate. The possibilities are endless and, in my humble opinion, exciting. There are obviously limitations in different school settings in terms of access to computers/devices that allow students to complete and submit work electronically, and these can make this option of marking not viable for all.

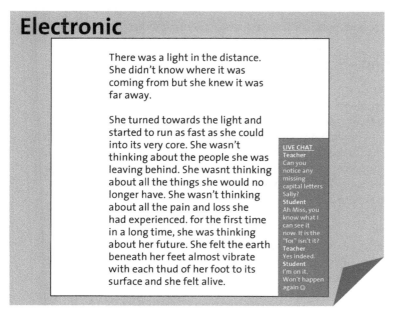

Fig. 13 Examples of marking – Electronic

Strengths:

There are several strengths for this approach to marking and feedback, e.g. long-term portfolios are easy to form for students; parents can have access; no lugging piles of books around to mark. In practical terms in the classroom, live marking is possible without interrupting students as they work therefore saving everyone time, and changes that are made in response to feedback are often trackable therefore showing the progress students are making.

Weaknesses:

Students need to have access to reliable technology in order to use these tools regularly.

When you might use it:

This approach is particularly powerful when students are working independently and you are able to access their work while they are actually completing it and offer feedback before they finish.

Student input:

Live marking while students are working is an exciting and hugely developmental tool. Students respond extremely well to this type of marking and they really enjoy it. Even just seeing your teacher icon pop up on their screen while they work makes them work harder. Giving them feedback while they are busy working away and then seeing them correct their errors live is powerful and satisfying for both teachers and students. You must try this!

Prompting – Scaffolding

Overview:

Prompting students on the necessary steps to take for improvement is really useful at all levels and can be used to ensure feedback is embedded and immediately acted upon to show progress and allow the student to rework their incorrect ideas or conceptions. One example of a useful prompt in the marking and feedback processes is a scaffold. This may involve giving a sentence starter or a fill in the gaps cloze activity for the student to complete to show they understand how to correct their work.

Strengths:

This approach ensures that students are acting upon marking and feedback straight away and in the manner that you want them to.

Weaknesses:

It could be seen as limiting that you are providing them with the start to a response rather than making them develop it independently.

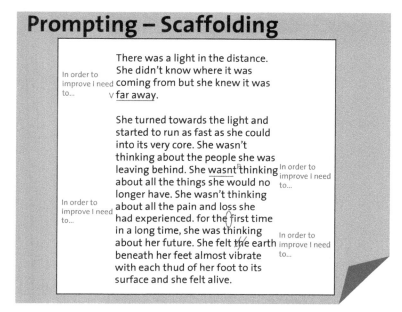

Prompting – Scaffolding

There was a light in the distance. She didn't know where it was coming from but she knew it was ~~far away~~. v far away.

In order to improve I need to...

She turned towards the light and started to run as fast as she could into its very core. She wasn't thinking about the people she was leaving behind. She wasnt thinking about all the things she would no longer have. She wasn't thinking about all the pain and loss she had experienced. for the first time in a long time, she was thinking about her future. She felt the earth beneath her feet almost vibrate with each thud of her foot to its surface and she felt alive.

In order to improve I need to...

In order to improve I need to...

In order to improve I need to...

Fig. 14 Examples of marking – Prompting – Scaffolding

When you might use it:
When students are really struggling due to a lack of confidence, this can give them a platform to climb from.

Student input:
It is important to emphasise to students how important it is to use or adapt your scaffold to take steps to improve their work as soon as possible and to make sure they bear the comment in mind next time they have a similar task.

Prompting – Example

Overview:
Example prompts used in marking and feedback can include the teacher showing or providing an example of what is needed for improvement and asking the student to produce a similar piece, looking at their own first draft and the example to guide them on how to improve. Students seeing an example of what they have produced, but perhaps a level or two above what they created, can be helped to jump up to meet the next level of expectations and bring to life what that actually looks like.

Prompting – Example

> Instead of "far away" you could consider using the phrase "a lifetime away from where she was right now."
>
> There was a light in the distance. She didn't know where it was coming from but she knew it was far away.
>
> She turned towards the light and started to run as fast as she could into it's very core. She wasn't thinking about the people she was leaving behind. She _wasnt_ thinking about all the things she would no longer have. She wasn't thinking about all the pain and loss she had experienced. for the first time in a long time, she was thinking about her future. She felt the earth beneath her feet almost vibrate with each thud of her foot to it's surface and she felt alive.
>
> Change wasnt for wasn't

Fig. 15 Examples of marking – Prompting – Example

Strengths:

Example prompts allow students to see a clear example of exactly what you are looking for, and they are then able to compare their own work to it. They can then try and emulate what they see in their own work.

Weaknesses:

Some students can be stifled by examples of great work; it can knock their confidence if they see something so far above what they are currently doing. It can also lead to copying rather than using the example as inspiration.

When you might use it:

When you want students to aspire to be the very best, then give them the very best to look at.

Student input:

Making sure you talk through the examples you provide to students will ensure that they can engage with them. Students need to be taught how to break down the example and apply and compare it to their own work.

Prompting – Reminder

Overview:

Reminder prompts in marking and feedback will often take the form of questions to prompt memory of prior learning or content covered in class. They remind the students of the intention, assessment focuses, skills involved, knowledge to be shown and the prior learning involved in the creation of the particular piece of work. This is a great tool to get students thinking and linking back to prior learning. Best practice includes space for the student to respond to the prompts in and around the piece of work, and will lead to them reworking their piece with these prompts kept in mind and acted upon.

Strengths:

This approach gets the students to connect with prior learning and think for themselves about what they have missed out or not done well enough rather than telling them straight away.

Weaknesses:

Some students may not be able to recall what you want them to from your prompt and may need further assistance.

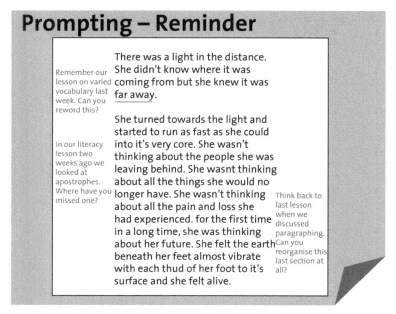

Fig. 16 Examples of marking – Prompting – Reminder

When you might use it:

If you are revisiting a skill, or some knowledge learnt earlier in the year, and want your students to connect that learning together and then work through the issue independently.

Student input:

With this approach, students are forced to think and look back to work they have done previously. It is important to ensure that the prior work is clearly labelled so that students can refer back with clarity.

Holistic

Overview:

Holistic marking and feedback involves the teacher reading the entire piece of work and only giving marking and feedback at the end. The teacher will provide comments on the work and possible improvements in the form of prose. The prose will be directed at the student and discuss the work produced.

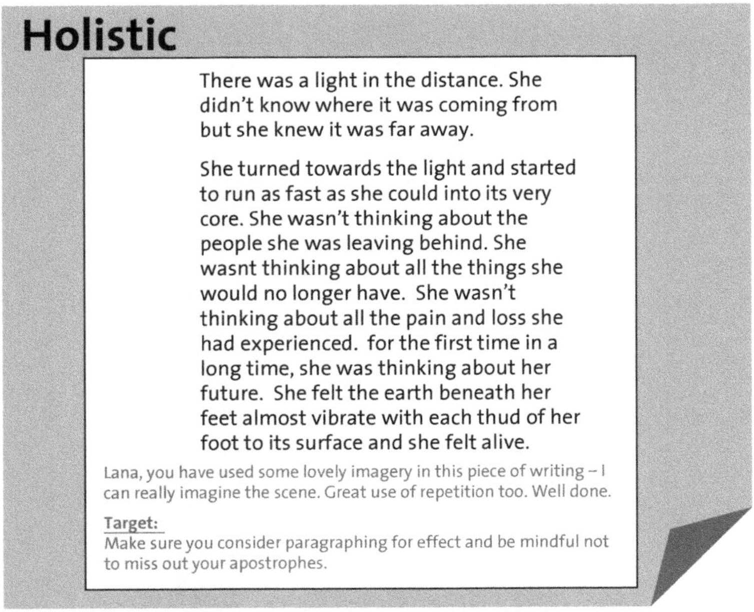

Holistic

There was a light in the distance. She didn't know where it was coming from but she knew it was far away.

She turned towards the light and started to run as fast as she could into its very core. She wasn't thinking about the people she was leaving behind. She wasnt thinking about all the things she would no longer have. She wasn't thinking about all the pain and loss she had experienced. for the first time in a long time, she was thinking about her future. She felt the earth beneath her feet almost vibrate with each thud of her foot to its surface and she felt alive.

Lana, you have used some lovely imagery in this piece of writing – I can really imagine the scene. Great use of repetition too. Well done.

Target:
Make sure you consider paragraphing for effect and be mindful not to miss out your apostrophes.

Fig. 17 Examples of marking – Holistic

Strengths:

The marking load can be more manageable for the teacher as they only have to summarise their findings and advice once rather than all the way through the marking process.

Weaknesses:

This type of marking can be overwhelming or confusing for some students as they are unable to clearly see the areas you are commenting on, and are therefore not clear on what to improve.

When you might use it:

Perhaps when marking the second draft of a particular piece of work when the students are very familiar with what they have produced.

Student input:

Students are given personalised extended feedback which will allow them to think deeply about their work and also feel appreciated. It is a good idea to get them to respond to your comments in similar prose to that which you have used to give them feedback.

Rapid response

Overview:

Rapid response can be used alongside any other marking and feedback approach. It merely means that the student is to respond rapidly to the marking and feedback that has been provided to them. This usually takes place as soon after the work has been completed as possible, so the work is still fresh in the student's memory. This may involve the student writing a response to a question you posed, rewriting a section or all of the work with the feedback and marking in mind or completing a set task to show progress in a skill that was lacking.

Strengths:

Students are forced to think about and act upon the feedback that has been provided to them while they work and their reading of the feedback is fresh in their mind. This could help some students retain the full learning and knowledge that is possible from the feedback given.

Weaknesses:

It can be quite time-consuming, as lesson time will have to be scheduled in and planned to specifically allow for this.

Rapid response

> There was a light in the distance. She didn't know where it was coming from but she knew it was far away.
>
> She turned towards the light and started to run as fast as she could into its very core. She wasn't thinking about the people she was leaving behind. She wasnt thinking about all the things she would no longer have. She wasn't thinking about all the pain and loss she had experienced. for the first time in a long time, she was thinking about her future. She felt the earth beneath her feet almost vibrate with each thud of her foot to its surface and she felt alive.

Lana, you have used some lovely imagery in this piece of writing – I can really imagine the scene. Great use of repetition too. Well done.

Target:
Make sure you consider paragraphing for effect and be mindful not to miss out your apostrophes.

Task:
Rewrite this piece, making sure to include any corrections. You must act upon any advice you have been given by me too.

Fig. 18 Examples of marking – Rapid response

When you might use it:

Whenever you have marked a piece of work and provided feedback. If you have bothered to mark and give feedback on a piece of work then it is essential that you give time and space for students to review, think and act upon it.

Student input:

Students are forced to respond straight away while work is fresh in their minds. Getting them to do this so soon after completing the initial task encourages mastery and makes honing their work and aiming high a norm.

Questions

Overview:

Using questions for marking and feedback can really prompt students to think about the key components of the task that was completed. Through your questions you are feeding back on areas you want them to improve on, but not giving them all the answers – they have to question themselves first.

Questions

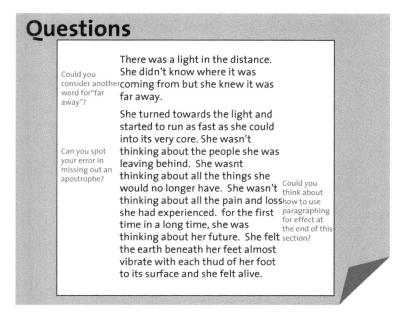

Could you consider another word for "far away"?

There was a light in the distance. She didn't know where it was coming from but she knew it was far away.

Can you spot your error in missing out an apostrophe?

She turned towards the light and started to run as fast as she could into its very core. She wasn't thinking about the people she was leaving behind. She wasnt thinking about all the things she would no longer have. She wasn't thinking about all the pain and loss she had experienced. for the first time in a long time, she was thinking about her future. She felt the earth beneath her feet almost vibrate with each thud of her foot to its surface and she felt alive.

Could you think about how to use paragraphing for effect at the end of this section?

Fig. 19 Examples of marking – Questions

Strengths:
Marking using questions and only questions is a great way to get the students involved in the marking process.

Weaknesses:
This approach may not work for students if there are clear gaps in their knowledge.

When you might use it:
When you are confident that students have the background knowledge necessary but have simply missed out elements that could really help them to progress.

Student input:
Instead of just being given advice and guidance, students are made to think deeply and question their own skills and knowledge. They are encouraged to come to their own conclusion and perhaps find more within themselves than they thought possible.

Encouragement

Overview:

Including encouragement in your marking and feedback can be motivational and spur students on by building their confidence in their own abilities. Encouragement can take the form of a simple tick, smiley face or sticker. It can also include compliments on skills that are well-developed or knowledge that is well-expressed. Who doesn't want to feel appreciated when they have worked hard on something?

Strengths:

It can build confidence in areas that deserve celebration in student work. Students need boosting and this is always a positive thing if the boost is a valid one.

Weaknesses:

A word of warning: if overused this type of marking and feedback can lose all impact and even be detrimental to the student by over-building their confidence when improvements are still necessary.

When you might use it:

Praise where praise is due.

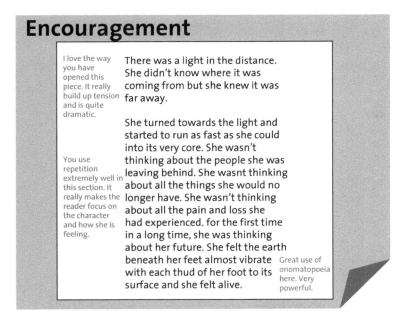

Fig. 20 Examples of marking – Encouragement

Student input:

Students will be guided to look at the things they have done well and feel proud of their efforts. They will be more likely to continue doing those things they do well if they are praised for them.

Targets

Overview:

Clear and specific targets given at the end of a piece of work can be very useful for students. Ideally these targets should be taken from assessment focuses that the students are familiar with and that had been shared and discussed prior to completing the task. The targets need to be challenging while still being accessible. Students will often need specific next steps along with targets so that they know what action will help them progress in this area. Make sure that you choose targets that will have an impact and progress the students in their learning. Ensure that you don't give too many targets at once; choose the targets that will make a difference.

Targets

There was a light in the distance. She didn't know where it was coming from but she knew it was far away.

She turned towards the light and started to run as fast as she could into its very core. She wasn't thinking about the people she was leaving behind. She wasnt thinking about all the things she would no longer have. She wasn't thinking about all the pain and loss she had experienced. for the first time in a long time, she was thinking about her future. She felt the earth beneath her feet almost vibrate with each thud of her foot to its surface and she felt alive.

Targets:
- Make sure you consider paragraphing for effect.
- Be mindful not to miss out your apostrophes.

Fig. 21 Examples of marking – Targets

Strengths:

Students know simply and clearly exactly what they can do to move forward in their learning.

Weaknesses:

Students could focus solely on the targets you have given them and ignore any other corrections or improvements that are possible for that piece of work.

When you might use it:

When you have already made students familiar with the assessment or learning focuses for a piece of work.

Student input:

Students will be able to take immediate and focused action as a result of reading your targets.

Peer- and self-assessment

Overview:

When it comes to handing the marking process over to the students, it is essential that students have seen, discussed and practised using plenty of good models of marking and feedback. They see your marking all the time so make sure you are discussing the processes and how you mark with them – this is helpful for them understanding your feedback but also helps them to feedback well themselves. Don't expect students to be good at peer- or self-marking immediately – it takes time. Give them feedback on their feedback as you would a normal piece of work and soon they will begin to master the process. They need to know the assessment focuses well, but then this too is essential for them understanding your marking and feedback too, so there is no extra work there really! Giving them sentence starters for good feedback can help. Offering guidance such as being kind, honest and specific can also be helpful. Using a specific colour for student-led marking can help you, and them, easily see their attempts and if they are improving over time in their books with the marking process.

Strengths:

Students have a better understanding of the marking criteria for work they are producing for you and therefore how to improve their own work. Students will have a deeper understanding of the marking and feedback that you provide for them also.

Weaknesses:

Time and training during lesson time is essential prior to the students taking part in peer- or self-assessment. The training process needs to be revisited and honed regularly with the students in order for it to have impact.

When you might use it:

Only once you have given over plenty of in-class training time to the students for understanding and practising the process.

Student input:

Students take full ownership of improving their own work and the work of others. They are made to think about the success criteria in detail and apply them. This means that they are gaining a deeper understanding of the task and what it takes to improve.

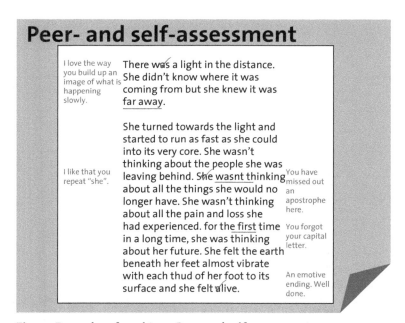

Fig. 22 Examples of marking – Peer- and self-assessment

Type of marking	Explanation	Average time to mark 30 books
1. Close	Close marking and feedback is detailed and in-depth marking. It involves a thorough read of the work with annotations of the content.	300 minutes
2. Focused	One particular assessment focus is chosen and that and that alone is marked in the student work.	90 minutes
3. Selective	Teacher selects a particular section of work produced to mark in depth (such as the introduction or conclusion) but leaves the rest unmarked.	90 minutes
4. Incorrect red herring	Teacher marks student's work as normal but places one incorrectly-marked comment into the mix as a red herring.	150 minutes
5. Coding	Teacher uses codes to mark students' work and the students write out the corresponding comment using that code to guide them.	105 minutes
6. Verbal	Teacher circulates while students work and gives verbal feedback that students write into their books immediately verbatim.	60 minutes
7. Electronic	Marking electronically-submitted work electronically.	75 minutes
8. Prompting– Scaffolding	Providing students with the structures or starter sentence they need to progress allowing them a step up to achieving success.	105 minutes
9. Prompting– Example	Showing and guiding students through three different level examples depending on their grade given after summative marking.	30 minutes
10. Prompting– Reminder	Reminders written on students' work to prompt memory of prior learning.	105 minutes
11. Holistic	All marking and feedback is written in prose at the end of the piece of work rather than all the way through.	150 minutes
12. Rapid response	Getting students to respond to your marking as soon as you give it back to them.	20 minutes
13. Questions	Including questions at the end of students' work to encourage thinking about their learning and how to progress.	120 minutes
14. Encouragement	Including encouraging comments on students' work.	120 minutes
15. Targets	Specific, focused and clear targets given at the end of the piece of assessed work.	120 minutes
16. Self-and peer-assessment	Students taking control of the marking process once they have been trained by you.	10 minutes

Fig. 23 Overview of the different approaches to marking and feedback

Chapter 3 takeaway

Teaching tip

Make your marking manageable

Consider the work you are setting that will need to be marked and set it purposefully. Allocate time to mark that work and apply a strategy to your marking such as focusing only on certain skills or sections if necessary to be able to get through it. Good intentions are great but no use if they are impossible to achieve. Time is precious in teaching so make sure you plan out what you are going to do and get it done in that time frame. Be kind to yourself and remain realistic.

Pass it on

Sharing your ideas – Colleagues outside your school setting

Sharing your ideas and experience in marking and feedback with colleagues outside of your school setting can be a real eye-opener. We are often so busy as teachers that we don't realise that we are stuck in our own little bubble and don't look outside it to see what else there is and how we could approach things differently. This is partly because we have so little time to spare. But sharing and finding excellent practice is essential, so it is not something we can just ignore. It can save us all time in the long run if we become better at what we do by working with, and sharing with, other colleagues both within and outside of our classrooms, departments and schools.

Many schools now have official links with other schools due to being part of an academy chain or being overseen by a regional council. This is great for sharing good practice as there are often already systems in place to do this. There are also now many organisations that work specifically on projects that link schools together and this too works well for sharing good practice. If you are not officially linked to another school, there is nothing stopping you initiating the process yourself. How about linking up with a department or colleague outside of your setting and sharing good practice? There are many ways you could share good practice across schools, such as having phone contact with a link colleague in another school; setting up exchange days where two colleagues link and take a day with each other in their respective schools experiencing life outside their own school setting; organising a TeachMeet; overseeing a cross-school project either with staff, students or both and hosting CPD evening sessions with other schools.

Sharing with staff in your school
Suggest a sharing slot in your whole-school morning meeting once a week and share a marking experience with them. You could discuss your positive experience with one of the types of marking in this chapter. It could well spark the teaching and learning discussion at the coffee machine for that week.

Share and tweet
Share your experiences with different types of marking and feedback approaches in your classroom on Twitter using the hashtag #BloomsCPD.

CPD book club recommendation

Robert Rosenthal and Lenore Jacobson, *Pygmalion in the Classroom* (See Bibliography and further reading, page 295)

Bloggers' corner

Sarah Findlater (yes me!) has some good posts on marking and feedback including digital marking and feedback that are well worth a read.
Visit my blog at http://msfindlater.blogspot.co.uk

TO DO LIST:

- ☐ Reflect on different marking and feedback approaches that you use now or have used in the past and consider your successes and failures with them
- ☐ Tweet your experiences with different types of marking and feedback approaches and check out what others have said by using the hashtag #BloomsCPD
- ☐ Suggest a weekly marking and feedback sharing slot at your whole school morning meetings
- ☐ Check out Sarah Findlater's blog posts on marking and feedback http://msfindlater.blogspot.co.uk
- ☐ Read *Pygmalion in the Classroom* by Robert Rosenthal and Lenore Jacobson

4 Getting to grips with the big ideas

There are many great thinkers out there who have conducted research and opened dialogue about important educational issues with a wider audience than ever before. To be honest, there is perhaps too much for us teachers to have the time to take in. Below are a few of the ideas relevant to marking and feedback specifically that have been explored through educational research and discussions. The studies and ideas are not explored in full, as that would be a whole other book or series of books, but they are instead dipped into and then linked to the key areas that we are focusing on in this book. Further reading on each person and study is highly recommended as they are all very different and make fascinating reading. Links are provided for the ongoing research by each person and on each idea referenced.

Throughout this chapter, after describing each writer's 'big ideas', I suggest some takeaway ideas for you to explore using in your own classroom – these are simple strategies inspired by the research and which work brilliantly. You can dip in to these ideas and try them out individually, or combine them, as you will be shown in the next chapter (see Chapter 5, p.83). For ease of cross-reference, therefore, the strategies described in the takeaway ideas are numbered consecutively and summarised for quick-reference at the end of the chapter (p.79).

Writer/researcher	Specialist area	Key publication	Website	Twitter handle
Dylan Wiliam	Assessment and feedback	*Inside the Black Box*	www.dylanwiliam.org	@dylan wiliam
John Hattie	Feedback	*Visible Learning for Teachers*	www.visiblelearningplus.com	N/a
Carol Dweck	Mindset	*Mindset*	mindsetonline.com	N/a
Robert Rosenthal and Lenore Jacobson	High expectations	*Pygmalion in the Classroom*	www.youtube.com/watch?v=hTghEXKNj7g	N/a
Doug Lemov	Teaching techniques and practice	*Teach Like a Champion*	teachlikeachampion.com	@Doug_Lemov
Daniel T. Willingham	Cognitive science	*Why Don't Students Like School?*	www.danielwillingham.com	@DTWillingham
Ron Berger	Excellence	*An Ethic of Excellence*	vimeo.com/21983525	@RonBergerEL
Robert Bjork	Desirable difficulties	N/a	bjorklab.psych.ucla.edu	N/a

Fig. 24 Making and feedback – the big ideas

Dylan Wiliam on Assessment and feedback

Name: Dylan Wiliam

Twitter handle: @dylanwiliam

Website: www.dylanwiliam.org

What to read: *Inside the Black Box* by Dylan Wiliam and Paul Black

What to watch: www.journeytoexcellence.org.uk/resourcesandcpd/biographies/biogdylanwiliam.asp

---

In a series of recorded talks, Wiliam discusses his ideas on assessment and feedback (See *What to watch* above). In his talk on 'Feedback on learning', he describes feedback as either being 'ego-involving' or 'task-involving'.

- 'Ego-involving' feedback includes giving generalised praise to students or allocating grades for work resulting in students comparing themselves with others in the class.
- 'Task-involving' feedback focuses more on steps for improvement in that particular task and how students might go about this.

Wiliam explains that psychological studies have shown that 'ego-involving' feedback is 'rarely' effective, and at times can even have a 'negative effect', actually lowering achievement. He argues that it is possibly better to say nothing than to give this type of feedback to students. On the other hand, task-involving feedback was shown to have a significantly positive impact on student achievement.

Wiliam urges teachers to ensure that they are aware of the importance of the student's response to getting feedback. He emphasises the need to train students and create an environment where their first action when feedback is given is to think about it and not react emotionally. If students do react emotionally it can be to be defensive and can lead to possible disengagement. An emotional reaction takes the students' thinking away from the learning and deep into the emotional response, the gut instinct to protect themselves and their own well-being.

'When they're faced with a task or a response to a piece of work, students, basically, make a choice between deciding either to protect their well-being or to engage in activities that will actually help them grow as individuals.' (Dylan Wiliam, 'Feedback on learning' video)

In his talk on 'Self- and peer-assessment', Wiliam makes a clear distinction between summative and formative peer- and self-assessment:

- In summative peer- and self- assessment, the students are essentially marking the work so that teachers do not have to.
- In formative peer- and self-assessment, students are helping one another to improve their work.

He says that in studies he conducted, it was clear that formative peer- and self-assessment has reciprocal benefits for both the assessor and the assessed. For both approaches, it helps students because they are forced to internalise the success criteria in the context of a piece of work. For peer-assessment, he noticed that when students had conducted peer-assessment, their own subsequent work in that same area was often much improved as they were clearer about the expectations. Peer-assessment also has the benefit of having a less emotional response as it is someone else's work.

Putting it into practice

Below are some simple strategies that have been inspired by Dylan Wiliam's ideas described above. Try them out and see what you think. Adapt them where you see fit.

Strategy 1: No grades

Taking the above into consideration, look at your marking and assessing and evaluate whether you give more 'task-involving' or 'ego-involving' feedback. Which do you find has more impact in your students' books? Do you use grades too often?

You could consider not providing students with grades or withholding them until certain points during the year. If you are required to grade, is there a way you could withhold the grades and ask students to act upon your feedback before you let them know their grade?

Strategy 2: Target banks

Form a bank of targets based on the specific assessment focuses for the topic you are studying with your class. You can do this very easily by breaking down the skills you want the students to be using by the end of the unit and then creating a target for each level of mastery: basic, middle and advanced, as appropriate for your students. You can form a grid to easily display the targets with the skills along the top and the level of mastery along the side. This will make task-involving feedback really easy with your students and speed up your marking process as you can just select and drop in the relevant target for each piece of marking.

It is a good idea to discuss and familiarise the students with this bank of targets and how they change as the students move through the levels of mastery, so that they recognise them when they are getting their feedback. You can even form a code for each target and allocate the code on the piece of work and get the students to write the target out themselves using the target grid. Short, specific and familiar targets that are task-involving with clear steps forward are great for getting students to move forward in their learning.

Strategy 3: Student marking

Reflect on your current peer- and self-assessment processes. What is working and what is not? Why is that? Have you shared the success criteria and allowed them to access it enough to complete this process effectively? If not, how can you do this?

You could look at making peer- and self-marking a regular slot in your lessons to get the students used to and well-practised in the skill. I have always found that you need to train the students well in this art to get good results. Training takes time and needs clear and detailed instruction with examples given. I often mark a piece of work live on the interactive whiteboard before I set them off on the task. I talk through my thinking to allow them to see both how I approach the process and how to mark effectively.

John Hattie on Feedback

Name: John Hattie

Website: www.visiblelearningplus.com

What to read: *Visible Learning for Teachers* by John Hattie; *Feedback in schools* (*Chapter 18*) by John Hattie in *Feedback* edited by Robbie Sutton, Matthew Hornsey and Karen Douglas; 'Feedback in schools' (http://visible-learning.org/2013/10/john-hattie-article-about-feedback-in-schools)

John Hattie has focused on feedback in much of his extensive research over the years. He found feedback to be one of the top ten influencers on student progress and achievement. He has explored many issues around feedback and highlights the following as some of the most important elements for success:

- quality over quantity
- positive student culture towards receiving feedback
- disconfirmation is more powerful than confirmation in feedback
- errors must be welcomed
- correct peer feedback is powerful
- assessments should provide teachers with feedback about their methods.

(John Hattie: *Feedback in schools* in *Feedback*)

Hattie talks of the importance of student expectation or student self-reported grades. He notes in his book, *Visible Learning for Teachers*, the importance of students being able to become aware of their own expectations on themselves and then encouraged to exceed these in order to ensure motivation and subsequent progression. He claims that students are very good a predicting what grade they will achieve in any given test, but that the teacher's job is to push them further to *'exceed their potential'.*

Hattie emphasises the importance of formative evaluation procedures both before and during the learning process. He also mentions the importance of feedback from student to teacher as this allows the teacher to see the learning through the eyes of the student, making learning visible and allowing next steps to be planned.

Putting it into practice

Below are some simple strategies that have been inspired by John Hattie's ideas explored above. Try them out and see what you think. Adapt them where you see fit.

Strategy 4: Less is more

Consider whether you focus too much on 'getting your marking done' and showing that you mark regularly. Consider marking less often but in more depth or with a sharper focus. It would be a better use of your time and you would see more of an impact with your students. Share the approach you are taking with the students and keep it structured. Make marking and feedback an event and really give it the focus it deserves.

Strategy 5: Student approach

How do your students currently respond to your marking and feedback when they receive it? You could consider holding some discussion sessions covering the point of marking and how best to approach it. Train your students to respond to marking and feedback as they should – a developmental process and not merely a criticism.

Do your students have high expectations of themselves and know how to achieve and exceed these expectations? If not, make sure you provide them with the tools to do this in your classroom.

Strategy 6: Peer feedback

Once you train the students to fully understand your marking and how it is done, they will be able to mark one another's work to a much higher standard. Students can often take on board more from a peer that they are on a level with than a teacher, so if we allow them to give peer feedback we must make sure we have trained them to give that feedback well.

Strategy 7: Welcome failure

Encourage an open attitude to being wrong. Students learn more from their errors than from all the things they are getting right. Encourage them to focus on what they are getting wrong and the targets for improvement that are linked to those errors that you have highlighted in your marking and feedback.

Strategy 8: Student–teacher feedback

Do your assessments, both formative and summative, feed directly into your teaching? Do you adapt in line with your students? If they are not grasping any particular concept, are you aware and have you tried other approaches to the topic or problem? Make sure you listen to your students, are responsive to them and adapt as you go.

Carol Dweck on Mindset

Name: Carol Dweck
Website: mindsetonline.com
What to read: *Mindset* by Carol Dweck

Carol Dweck explores the idea of 'growth mindsets' and 'fixed mindsets' in her work.

- In essence, a 'fixed mindset' is one that believes intelligence is fixed.
- A 'growth mindset' is one that sees intelligence as something that can be developed.

Someone with a 'fixed mindset' has the desire to prove themselves over and over again. They take criticism as an attack on their character and believe it should be avoided. They are often threatened by the success of others and can opt to stop trying rather than face the possibility of failing.

Someone with a 'growth mindset' would embrace the process of learning and effort and would be driven to learn and practise in order to improve and they will preserve through hard times. They believe criticism is a valuable form of feedback and happily embrace it. Carol Dweck advocates the importance and impact cultivating growth mindsets can have.

> 'For students of a growth mindset, it doesn't make sense to stop trying. For them, adolescence is a time of opportunity: a time to learn new subjects'
> (Carol Dweck, *Mindset*)

Putting it into practice

Below are some simple strategies that have been inspired by the big ideas explored above. Try them out and see what you think. Adapt them where you see fit.

Strategy 9: Student mindset

Think of the students in your class. Who are your growth mindset students and who are your fixed mindset students? Conduct some debates and activities with your class to see how telling their responses are in terms of their approach to the task or the discussion topic. Do they display the growth mindset or fixed mindset?

Strategy 10: Marking mindset

Watch students' responses to your marking and feedback and see if you can spot those that can take the feedback well and those that cannot. What can you do to steer all students towards having a growth mindset when approaching the marking and feedback that they receive in school? Have open discussions with your students about these mindsets and the benefits of trying to foster a growth mindset.

Robert Rosenthal and Lenore Jacobson on High expectations

Name: Robert Rosenthal and Lenore Jacobson
What to read: *Pygmalion in the Classroom* by Robert Rosenthal and Lenore Jacobson
What to watch: 'The Pygmalion effect and the power of positive expectations' (www.youtube.com/watch?v=hTghEXKNj7g)

The Pygmalion effect is the phenomenon whereby the greater the expectation teachers place upon students, the better they perform. The name is taken from the Greek myth, *Pygmalion*, the story of a sculptor who fell in love with a statue he carved.

Robert Rosenthal and Lenore Jacobson conducted a study where they showed that if teachers were led to expect enhanced performance from students then the students' performance did indeed appear to enhance.

They took one elementary school and conducted an IQ test that only they were privy to the answers of – the information being withheld from the teachers. They then picked about 20% of the students at random and told their teachers that they were expected to be the gifted and talented students that would excel in comparison to their classmates. At the end of the study, all of the students did the same IQ test to check their progress. All groups of students showed some progress. However there was a statistically significant group of students in some of the lower year groups tested that showed the named gifted and talented students, whose teachers were told they should excel, made higher gains that other groups of students in their year.

> *'The change in the teachers' expectations regarding the intellectual performance of these allegedly 'special' children had led to an actual change*

in the intellectual performance of these randomly selected children.'
(Robert Rosenthal and Lenore Jacobson, *Pygmalion in the classroom*)

This led to the conclusion that teacher expectation, especially with younger students, can indeed influence student achievement. Through their study they explored the notion that reality can be influenced positively or negatively by the expectations of others. Rosenthal talks about biased expectancies affecting reality and creating self-fulfilling prophecies.

Putting it into practice

Below are some simple strategies that have been inspired by Robert Rosenthal and Lenore Jacobson's research described above. Try them out and see what you think. Adapt them where you see fit.

Strategy 11: High expectations

Do you have high expectations for all your students all of the time? Really? Take the time to think about how you approach all of the students in your class individually. Do you build their self-belief through your marking and feedback? Are your targets and comments encouraging them to keep reaching higher and move themselves forward? Do you make them *all* feel like they have something to give? You create the climate in your classroom, so harness that power for good and keep your marking and feedback aspirational for all your students, all of the time.

Doug Lemov on Teaching techniques and practice

Name: Doug Lemov

Twitter handle: @Doug_Lemov

Website: teachlikeachampion.com

What to read: *Teach Like a Champion* by Doug Lemov, *Practice Perfect* by Doug Lemov, Erica Woolway and Katie Yezzi

---

Doug Lemov believes that great teaching is an art. In his book, *Teach Like a Champion* he sets out the 62 techniques he believes make the difference between good teaching and great teaching. He has based these techniques on his observations of highly effective teachers. The techniques are all concrete and actionable, allowing teachers to use them in their classroom immediately.

A selection of the techniques he recommends are outlined below:

- No opt out – students must provide an answer to questions asked even if it means getting help.

- Right is right – never accept a wrong answer; only the exact answer you were looking for is the right answer.
- Format matters – how students say something is just as important as what they are saying.
- Begin with the end – when planning, teachers start with the end-game in mind and form the lesson around working towards achieving the objective.
- Break it down – when presenting material to students make sure that it is clear and each element is broken down into component parts.
- Do it again – doing it again and doing it right, better or perfect.
- Precise praise – ensure that praise is precise and used when it is deserved.
- Normalise error – make getting it wrong OK in your classroom; it is all part of the journey.

He emphasises that the ideas he sets out are not glamorous but they work.

> *'One of the problems with teaching is that there's a temptation to evaluate what we do in the classroom based on how clever it is... not necessarily how effective it is in driving student achievement.'*
> (Doug Lemov, *Teach Like a Champion*)

Another of Lemov's books, *Practice Perfect* (written alongside Erica Woolway and Katie Yezzi) discusses the topic of what makes practising something have the most impact. He argues that practice does not necessarily make perfect; practice makes permanent. He explores what makes us get better at things and the importance of practising the right things not the wrong things to improve. He uses examples from the classroom to illustrate the ideas in the book.

One example idea given is that of the approach to students misbehaving. According to Lemov, an 'ineffective' approach would be for the teacher to stop their instruction to verbally correct a student who is doing something wrong as it takes the focus from the teacher to the student. The 'effective' approach would be to use non-verbal correction (such as two fingers to the teacher eyes) to keep the focus on the teacher rather than the student. The more you approach the situation in an 'effective' manner, the better the focus in your classroom becomes. Full control of the class and the learning within the class is easy the more you practise the best way of doing something.

The book sets out 42 techniques for practising until you are perfect. It begins by exploring some false assumptions about practising, such as the belief that you only need to practise what you are not good at. Lemov believes that we need to practise the things we are good at just as much. The book then goes on to look at how to run effective practices such as the technique of isolating the skill – breaking practice down into discreet skills and perfecting them in a simple setting before taking them on to more complex settings. It also explores modelling techniques and the importance of explicit explanation when an expert is modelling something for others to learn and practise to become expert in. The book also discusses the importance of feedback and the fact that practice is a social activity needing openness, transparency and humility. He advocates a process of 'multiple rounds of practice, to let people practise, struggle, get feedback,and then try again' (Doug Lemov, Erica Woolway and Katie Yezzi, *Practice Perfect*) as well as the use of coaches when giving feedback, practising using feedback and acting upon feedback immediately.

Putting it into practice

Below are some simple strategies that have been inspired by Lemov's ideas described above. Try them out and see what you think. Adapt them where you see fit.

Strategy 12: Q & A (No opt out)

When marking, try posing developmental questions in your feedback that your students must answer underneath where you have written. If they don't know the answer then they need to find out. Give them the tools and resources necessary to help if they need it. Getting them to document this in their books in response to your marking is a great way to ensure they can see that they are progressing. (See Chapter 3, p.37)

Strategy 13: No 'nearly there' (Right is right/perfect practice)

Ensure that you never accept a 'nearly there' answer. Make your students work toward the correct answer at all times in your marking and feedback. Demand the highest input from them. If you do not correct an error because it is 'nearly there', however minor, then they will continue to practise these incorrect ways of thinking or working and get better at doing it wrong – no one wants that!

Strategy 14: Say what? (Format matters)

When you see instances of casual or incorrect expression in your students' work, make sure you correct it to the formal equivalent. There is never a reason to let it slide, even if you 'get what they mean'! Ask them to rephrase the sentence through your marking and feedback – on the spot and immediately when they get the marked work back.

Strategy 15: Eyes on the prize (Begin with the end)

When you are planning and leading class time where students are creating a piece of work that will be marked by you, ensure that you let them know exactly what you expect them to produce at the end of it. Model it.

Strategy 16: Chunk it up (Break it down/isolate the skill/explicit explanation)

When providing marking and feedback, make sure that the targets that you give are clear, specific and actionable for the students. If they need further explanation or learning, then provide that when they get the work back. Be mindful not to give comments or feedback that is too generalised, but instead break down exactly what they can do to make their work better. What couple of things could they do to really have impact in their work and make improvements?

Strategy 17: Rework it (do it again)

Give students regular opportunities to respond to your feedback, practise skills they need and gather any necessary knowledge, then make them do it again. The same, or a similar task, reworked can really have impact and make sure that students learn lessons from their errors. Foster a culture of craftsmanship and mastery in your students' work.

Strategy 18: Wrong is OK (normalise error)

Make getting it wrong OK in your classroom. When students get feedback, make sure that they are really embracing the errors they have made and working on them without feeling like they are failures. It takes time and encouragement, but get them thinking about being comfortable with being wrong in their work and see it as an opportunity to act upon your advice and feedback and get better quicker.

Strategy 19: Practise everything (Practice good, practice bad)

When you are marking and giving feedback to students make sure that you are encouraging them to keep practising the things they are good at, as well as those they are not so good at, so that all of their skills are being honed and kept well-oiled.

Daniel T. Willingham on Cognitive science

Name: Daniel T. Willingham
Twitter handle: @DTWillingham
Website: www.danielwillingham.com
What to read: *Why Don't Students Like School?* by Daniel T. Willingham

---

Daniel T. Willingham has written extensively about the importance of cognitive science in education. He argues that cognitive science has critical insights to teach us about how the mind works and consequently how we should use instruction in the classroom. In his book, *Why Don't Students Like School?*, he makes various recommendations for effective instruction such as focusing on long-term memory as it is almost unlimited; his view is that effective instruction should minimise overloading students' working short-term memory and maximise the use of their long-term memory.

In the same book, he discusses how vital it is to ensure that background knowledge is taught in order for critical thinking skills to be effectively learnt.

> *'Factual knowledge must precede skill... facts must be taught, ideally in the context of skills.'* (Daniel T. Willingham, *Why Don't Students Like School?*)

He also discusses the idea that memory is the residue to thought:

> *'[Teachers] must pay careful attention to what an assignment will actually make students think about... because that is what they will remember.'* (Daniel T. Willingham, *Why Don't Students Like School?*)

Therefore, we should be providing students with questions, problems, examples, stories and mnemonics to make learning memorable and really get them thinking. Designing our lessons, crafting the order of our content and ensuring that we are building skills on top of a solid knowledge foundation for learning to be long lasting and have impact.

Putting it into practice

Below are some simple strategies that have been inspired by Daniel T. Willingham's ideas explored above. Try them out and see what you think. Adapt them where you see fit.

Strategy 20: Background knowledge

When you are marking your students' work, do you get the impression that some students lack the background knowledge necessary to complete the task to a good level? If so, what can you provide them with to fill this gap?

Strategy 21: Think to remember

When you set a task that you will be marking, have you provided the students with high-quality examples to aim towards? Are there any stories or mnemonics that you could share with the students prior to the task being undertaken to enable them to remember the key skills and knowledge that will allow them to achieve well in the task? When marking and giving feedback, make sure that you are asking them questions and giving them space to answer those questions to develop their skills and knowledge in relation to the task completed. Can you provide them with a further task or problem that will extend their learning from the marked task?

Ron Berger on Excellence

Name: Ron Berger

Twitter handle: @RonBergerEL

What to read: *An Ethic of Excellence* by Ron Berger

What to watch: 'Doing good work' – the Ron Berger interview (www.youtube.com/watch?v=THfL7SYRcDU); 'Cultivating an ethic of excellence' (vimeo.com/21983525)

Ron Berger argues that high expectations play a vital role in improving student achievement. He uses the example of Austin's butterfly (https://www.youtube.com/watch?v=hqh1MRWZjms) to show the power of critique. He believes that we should have aspirational goals for all students at all times. He uses his experience as a carpenter to explore these ideas in his book, *An Ethic of Excellence*. He discusses the mastery and craftsmanship involved in carpentry and his belief that we need to develop classrooms full of craftsmen and women. He states that this approach would mean that students' work would be strong, accurate and beautiful and that they would be proud of their work regardless of their starting point or background.

> *'[A craftsman is] someone who has integrity and knowledge, who is dedicated to his work and who is proud of what he does and who he is. Someone who thinks carefully and does things well.'* (Ron Berger, *An Ethic of Excellence*)

Berger believes that in order to achieve excellence we need to ensure there is a whole-school culture of excellence where an ethic of excellence becomes the norm.

> *'[Excellence is] born from a culture'* (Ron Berger, *An Ethic of Excellence*)

Berger sets out five pedagogical principles that he believes help create a culture of excellence:

- assigning work that matters
- studying examples of excellence
- building a culture of kind, specific and helpful critique
- requiring multiple revisions and redrafts
- providing opportunities for public presentation.

Putting it into practice

Below are some simple strategies that have been inspired by Ron Berger's ideas explored above. Try them out and see what you think. Adapt them where you see fit.

Strategy 22: Make it matter

Ensure that when you are setting your students a task that will be marked by you, that you emphasise to the students the importance of the work. Make it matter to them and not just because you will be marking it. You could link it to the real world and how the skills are transferrable in real life, for example.

Strategy 23: Examples of excellence

Every time you are setting students off on a task for which they will be receiving your feedback, show them examples of excellence. Examples taken from other students are often the most powerful, but you can also look to books and the media.

Strategy 24: Student critique

Building a culture whereby students are able to give kind, specific and helpful critiques to one another starts with you. Make your marking follow this mantra; share the process with them and train them up to do it themselves.

Strategy 25: Revise and redraft

Ensure that you are including regular slots in your lessons for revision and redrafts as standard. When a piece of work has been marked, the student should expect to do it again and do it better – even if they have done well.

Strategy 26: Public presentation

Finding ways to celebrate and share excellent work is a wonderful thing to do with your students. You can, for instance, share great work with the rest of the class, display it on the classroom or hallway walls or host a presentation evening or afternoon for the school or families.

Robert Bjork on Desirable difficulties

Name: Robert Bjork

Website: bkjorklab.psych.ucla.edu

What to read: 'Desirable difficulties perspective on learning' (http://bjorklab.psych. ucla.edu/pubs/RBjork_inpress.pdf); Bjork Learning and Forgetting Lab Publications (http://bjorklab.psych.ucla.edu/RABjorkPublications.php)

Robert Bjork believes that certain training conditions that are difficult and can appear at first to slow down or impede performance, in fact have greater long-term benefits and better results in terms of achievement and progress. He believes that we need to focus more on long-term learning rather than performance he can see in the moment. Bjork has called these more difficult training conditions 'desirable difficulties.' Some of these desirable difficulties include:

- varying the conditions of learning rather than keeping them constant and predictable
- interleaving repetition of topics with different topics rather than grouping instruction
- spacing, rather than massing, study sessions on topics
- using tests over presentations as study events.

These particular difficulties are desirable, according to Bjork, because they encourage encoding and retrieval that in turn leads to learning, comprehension and remembering. He does also state that the learner needs a certain level of background knowledge in order for these difficulties to be truly desirable.

> '[If] a given learner is not equipped to overcome a difficulty that would otherwise be desirable, it becomes an undesirable difficulty... the learner must be equipped, by virtue of prior knowledge and current cues, to succeed... or it becomes an undesirable difficulty.' (Robert Bjork, 'Desirable difficulties perspective on learning')

Therefore we must ensure that our students have the ability to struggle with these difficulties in order for them to have impact and for students to experience progress.

Putting it into practice

Below are some simple strategies that have been inspired by the big ideas explored above. Try them out and see what you think. Adapt them where you see fit.

Strategy 27: Mix it up

Design your schedule of assessed work so that you provide opportunities to assess the same skill or knowledge with students but in multiple ways. Vary the conditions of learning but revisit the skill and/or knowledge often. Think of different tasks, activities, approaches and tests that you can conduct with your students to keep them on their toes and really embed the learning. The feedback you give to these tasks will ensure that progress is being made.

Strategy 28: Repeat and weave

Interweave repetition of learning into your planning. Instead of only marking and feeding back on specific skills and knowledge in isolation and once only, spread the learning and relearning of them over the term or year. Weave the same thread of learning along with other threads of learning so that the students are practising the skills and relearning the knowledge alongside other things. Make them look back over previous tasks and feedback that are linked so they can work on them again.

There are so many ways to approach marking and so many theories to consider. All of them have their place and you will have to experiment to find what works for you. The table below outlines the strategies that I use every day in my classroom and that I have found work and have real impact with the students.

Technique	Description
1. No grades	Withholding or not giving grades when you hand back marked student work.
2. Target banks	Using a bank of targets that marries up with your subject assessment objectives to draw from when you are marking student work.
3. Student marking	Getting students to mark their own work after adequate modelling and guided practice.
4. Less is more	Marking less often but in more depth.
5. Student approach	Developing student growth mindset when they approach your marking and feedback.
6. Peer feedback	Getting students to mark one another's work after adequate modelling and guided practice.
7. Welcome failure	Encouraging an open attitude to being wrong and learning from it.
8. Student–teacher feedback	Allowing your marking to inform your planning.
9. Student mindset	Becoming aware of the mindsets of your students.
10. Marking mindset	Noticing how students respond to your marking and encouraging them to have a growth mindset to help them engage with marking and feedback.
11. High expectations	Ensuring that you have high expectations in your marking and feedback comments at all times.
12. Q & A	Pose questions to your students in your marking to encourage deep reflection on their work.
13. No 'nearly there'	Ensure that you never accept a 'nearly there' answer in students' work.
14. Say what?	Insist on the correct grammar, vocabulary and phrasing in students' work through your marking and feedback.
15. Eyes on the prize	Show students exactly what you expect of their work before they begin and before you mark.
16. Chunk it up	Break down your feedback so that they can actually take it in. Do not overwhelm them.
17. Rework it	Make it the norm for students to revise and rework their work in your classroom on a regular basis.
18. Wrong is OK	Make getting it wrong in your classroom OK. Encourage risk-taking to develop students faster.
19. Practise everything	Make sure you are encouraging students to practise everything, including the things they are quite good at.
20. Background knowledge	Make sure that you fill in any necessary background knowledge that students may be lacking so that no student is at a disadvantage.
21. Think to remember	Make students really think as a result of your marking and feedback.
22. Make it matter	Make any work that you plan to mark really matter to them to get the best out of them.
23. Examples of excellence	Show your students examples of excellence prior to setting them off on a task that you intend to mark.
24. Student critique	Build a culture whereby students critiquing one another's work in a kind, specific and helpful manner is standard practice.
25. Revise and redraft	Plan out regular sessions when students are expected to revise and redraft their work for sustained periods of time.
26. Public presentation	Find ways to publicly celebrate student work as often as you can.
27. Mix it up	Design your schedule of assessed work so that you are assessing the same skills but in different ways.
28. Repeat and weave	Revisit topics, knowledge and skills regularly in your scheme of learning and assessment so that they are really embedded.

Fig. 25 Summary: marking strategies that work

Chapter 4 takeaway

Teaching tip

Make feedback a dialogue

Question your students when you mark their work, and leave space for them to respond to the questions posed. Get them thinking about their work and gave them the opportunity recognise their own errors and improve with your more subtle guidance. Rather than just saying 'do this', ask them questions that will lead them to do exactly what you want but also make them think in the process.

Pass it on

Sharing your ideas – Social media

There are many platforms, apps and tools that you can use in order to share good practice online. You can select the platform that suits your purpose and share with a small select group of people or the entire world and its wife. A good rule of thumb when it comes to using social media is to never post anything that you would not be happy with *anyone* seeing or reading: colleagues, family, students, managers, parents etc. If you do not already use one or all of these tools then make sure you take a leap of faith and try it out. You may well be surprised and like what you find.

Students on board

Try out some of the strategies mentioned in this chapter with your students. Discuss the strategies with them and ask their opinions. Making them a part of the marking process can be really useful when it comes to them interacting with your feedback. Explain the theory behind certain strategies you are using when feeding back to them. This will also make it much easier to start using peer-and self-assessment in class, as they will understand how to mark and feedback to achieve maximum impact.

Share and tweet

Share your thoughts on the ideas explored in this chapter or your experiences of using the strategies suggested on Twitter using the hashtag #BloomsCPD.

CPD book club recommendation

Carol Dweck, *Mindset*
(See Bibliography and further reading, page 295)

Bloggers' corner

Ross Morrison McGill has some interesting posts on marking and feedback
that are well worth a read. Visit his blog at http://teachertoolkit.me

TO DO LIST:

- [ ] Try out some of the strategies suggested in this chapter and see what works in your classroom
- [ ] Discuss the strategies you choose to use with your students and help them to understand the 'why' behind your marking and feedback practices
- [ ] Browse the websites, articles and videos shared in this chapter as and when you have time, or divide it up between colleagues and discuss them at meetings
- [ ] Get on Twitter and make sure you are following the people recommended in this chapter
- [ ] Tweet your thoughts on the ideas explored in this chapter or your experiences of using the strategies suggested and check out what others have said by using the hashtag #BloomsCPD
- [ ] Check out Ross Morrisson McGill's blog posts on marking and feedback: http://teachertoolkit.me
- [ ] Read *Mindset* by Carol Dweck

5 Putting it into practice

Having explored the different types of marking in Chapter 3 (page 37) and then looked at a wide range of different strategies for approaching marking and feedback in Chapter 4 (page 63), the purpose of this chapter is to develop ways of combining the individual strategies. A really powerful and systematic approach to marking and feedback incorporating lots of proven individual strategies in one smooth cyclical process has the potential to have a huge impact on progress, achievement and attainment in our classrooms.

The marking and feedback cycle

The model on the next page is one way, not the only way, of pulling together some of the takeaway approaches to marking and feedback that were shown to be effective in the last chapter. This model has been designed so that it can be applied to any age group, stage or subject across the curriculum. It naturally incorporates other areas of teaching and learning such as lesson planning and in-class instruction, as all good marking and feedback processes should. You can jump on the cycle wherever you see that it might work with your current practice and just follow the stages through.

Below are the details of each stage of the cycle and how you might apply them in the classroom. Each section suggests which of the takeaway marking and feedback strategies from Chapter 4 (page 63) you might like to implement at that particular point in the cycle. Obviously, each school, classroom, teacher and student are very different and you need to consider your own setting and adapt the process wherever you see fit.

Preparation

Case study

In her lesson, Mrs. Casey explains the task that will be taking place in detail, answering any questions that the students have. She shares with the students the mark scheme she is going to use to assess the work and conducts a highlighting activity where students highlight key words to help them understand the wording of the mark scheme. They then spend some time looking up any unfamiliar words in the mark scheme and Mrs. Casey holds a discussion on the mark scheme and how she uses it to mark their work. She then allows them to mark some sample work using the mark scheme and the class shares their work and discusses the mark scheme further.

This stage of the marking and feedback cycle essentially prepares the students for the task you are setting them and the subsequent marking and feedback they will receive in response to that piece of work.

Preparing students for the marking and feedback process is essential. Giving students the tools they need in order to succeed in a task will allow them to take

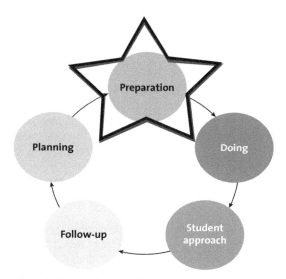

Fig: 26 The marking and feedback cycle

control and steer their learning in the direction you need them to go in; rather than being dragged along by you to the finish line. In order for this to happen, you need to carefully plan the activities and approach you take in the lead-up to the students completing the work you will mark and provide feedback on.

What do you need to think about?

When setting work that is going to be marked it is advisable to explicitly share with your students the fact that it will be an assessed piece of work and explain how you plan to assess the work they produce. This sounds obvious, but making this fact known to students and clearly setting out what is expected of them is so important that if missed out of the cycle then you are setting a large percentage of your students up for failure. They are not psychic and our job is to provide the guidance they need in order to succeed. Remember though, just because you are sharing success criteria with students does not mean you have to suck the joy out of a piece of work in the process. There are many ways you can remind, reinforce and check that students understand what they need to do in order to be successful in a task you are setting for them.

Which strategies might you like to use?

The strategies explored in the last chapter were discussed specifically in the context of marking and giving feedback to students, however, you can also use these approaches when you are preparing the students for marking and feedback too. Getting them used to the strategies in the lead-up to receiving marking and feedback on their work can take the fear out of the process, as they are practised in the approaches that you are taking. If, in your classroom practice, you mirror your marking and feedback practice then the students will connect with the marking and feedback with ease as they will hear *you* in the marking and feedback. It will be a familiar language to them and they will be able to act upon it effectively much more quickly.

- Strategy 22: Make it matter (p.77) When you are introducing a piece of work to your students that you plan to mark and provide feedback on, ensure that you build up the interest in that piece of work. You can make work matter by merely emphasising the fact that it will be assessed. But a more powerful approach is to make them care about the work they are producing. Make them care about the topic they are covering and inspire them to lose themselves in the work. Link the work to the real world or their interests or shape it around controversial issues.
- Strategy 20: Background knowledge (p.75) It is vital that the students' background knowledge is checked at this point rather than discovered after the task has been completed by them. If a student is missing vital background knowledge that will impact upon their approach to the task and ultimate success then it is our job to fill that gap. This allows all students to have the same chance of success regardless of their social background, cultural background or life experience.
- Strategy 15: Eyes on the prize (p.73) It is important that when students are approaching a lesson, sequence of lessons or the task itself, that they keep the end-game in mind. Share with students what you expect to see from them and provide them with real examples of the finished product and analyse them collaboratively to pull out what the example does well and how it does it.
- Strategy 23: Examples of excellence (p.77) Share with students exactly what you expect of them. Break down the techniques used and explore with the students the way that they can emulate that success in their own work.
- Strategy 11: High expectations (p.71) Make the students aspire to the very best and make them believe that they too can achieve excellence in their work if they work hard. When they are completing work in preparation for the assessed work, discussing in preparation of the assessed work or answering questions aloud in class, it is important to demand clear and formal expression from your students. If they can say it that way then they can write it that way; they just need your reassurance and practice to make them believe it themselves.
- Strategy 16: Chunk it up (p.74) Clear explanation of the task is essential for students to produce high quality work. Ensuring that you challenge students in terms of the content you explore with them, while also not overwhelming them, is the key to success here. Make sure that when you explain or present information to the students that it is bit by bit, not all at once. Checking that all students are on board with you and understand any skills or knowledge you convey to them will provide a firm foundation to the assessed work they will produce for you.

- Strategy 21: Think to remember (p.75) The final important element to the preparation stage of the marking and feedback cycle is to incorporate tasks in your preparation lesson or lessons that allow students to practise, using the skills and knowledge you need them to display in the assessed work you want them to complete. Make them really use their brains in the lessons leading up to the assessed work completion. Set tasks that get them thinking about different elements of the topic, skills and knowledge that they need to use. This will ensure that it stays fresh in their minds when they settle down to finally complete the task.
- Strategy 25: Revise and redraft (p.77) Give students plenty of short, sharp opportunities to redraft and revise skills in the preparation lesson or lessons so that they are really crafting the work they complete as standard practice. Get them taking pride in everything they complete in class. Make it the norm.
- Strategy 27: Mix it up (p.78) When covering the skills and knowledge they need in the assessed work make sure that you look at the same things from different angles to ensure students appreciate the complexity and depth of what you are covering. For instance, practise using a particular skill in different scenarios and then make the links between the different experiences they have had with that skill and what they noticed or learnt. Make the students masters in the skill before you begin to assess them in it.
- Strategy 7: Welcome failure (p.68) Finally, when students are practising using the skills and knowledge you want them to master, encourage bravery and risk. Make failure OK in your classroom; make it part of the journey to true success and mastery.

Once students are prepared well for work that you will be marking and feeding back on they will produce work that you will enjoy marking and they will be proud to hand in.

Key questions for reflection

1. Do you currently give students the tools they need in order to succeed in tasks you set?
2. Do you make the work that will be marked matter to your students?
3. Do you feel you explain tasks that will be marked well enough?
4. Do you show students examples of excellence so they know what they are aiming for?
5. Do you give your students chances to practise the skills needed in the assessed work?
6. Do your preparation tasks make students think deeply about the work they are producing?

Doing

Case study

The students move on to completing work that they know will be assessed by the same marking criteria that they have already used and broken down in class. The work is now marked by Mrs. Casey. She chooses to withhold grades and use the hierarchy of skill they have shared already as a class to represent their current position and give them targets. She chooses to use coding to mark their work and then also gives them one or two specific simple and high impact targets at the end of their piece of work. She chooses to phrase the targets as questions to make the students think more deeply about what she wants them to do to improve.

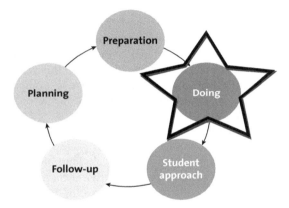

This stage of the marking and feedback cycle breaks down some useful techniques that teachers can incorporate into their marking and feedback time to ensure students are connecting with the feedback and progressing.

What do you need to think about?

Once students have completed the work that you have prepared them so well for, the task of actually getting down to it and doing the marking and feedback is all yours. The work will be of a high quality because they were well prepared for it in your lessons leading up to the completion of the piece of work. Now is the time to do it justice and provide high-quality, low-effort, high-impact marking and feedback that will enable your students to progress and improve. How you approach the marking will very much depend on the type of task the students have completed and what you are assessing but below are some key areas to consider when you are marking and giving feedback to your students.

Which strategies might you like to use?

- Strategy 1: No grades (p.66) You will have to decide whether it is appropriate for your students and the particular piece of work you are assessing to provide grades along with your feedback. If you are looking for impact then it is best to withhold or at least hold back grades until the marking and feedback has been digested and acted upon by the student. Your call at the end of the day.

- Strategy 4: Less is more (p.68) The feedback you give the students needs to be well-structured and clear in order for them to be able to get the most from it. Be selective and choose the skill or piece of knowledge that the student could improve upon that would make the most difference to the work and its quality. There may be a number of things that need improving but make the choice as to whether you need to point them all out this time or not. You know your students. Give them challenging feedback, yes, but make sure it is manageable for them to act upon. It is all very well telling them all the things that they need to improve, but if it is going to be too overwhelming for them all at once then the improvements may not get worked on, or indeed even thought about at all.
- Strategy 2: Target banks (p.66) The wording of the targets you give students in your feedback should also be considered carefully. You need to model the language you want them to use in terms of formality or subject-specific vocabulary. With this in mind, make sure you have trained your students well in understanding and using that language in advance of using it in feedback to them. It may be that you decide to use a bank of prewritten targets that the students have seen beforehand so that they are familiar. This also saves you time. This may not be appropriate or suitable for all tasks.
- Strategy 16: Chunk it up (p.74) However you choose to give targets to your students, make sure it is clear and actionable so that the student knows exactly what to do next in order to improve. Isolate the skill or knowledge that they need to work on and decide which you will ask them to work on to hone their focus. Take one step at a time and bear the individual student in mind when you are setting the targets.
- Strategy 11: High expectations (p.71) Keeping your expectations high when you are marking is vital to improving your students' self-belief. Making them believe that you believe they have it in them to do the very best should shine through in your marking and feedback at all times. Consider the way you are phrasing the feedback you are giving them. Make sure you are raising the bar at all times but also that you are not merely making them feel inadequate if they haven't quite got it.
- Strategy 14: Say what? (p.73) Making sure that you correct informal phrasing and grammatical errors is essential for your students to become the high-calibre scholars we all want them to be. Show them the correct phrasing and ensure they look back and use it in future speech and writing.
- Strategy 13: No 'nearly there' (p.73) If individual students have got something wrong, then make no excuses about saying that it is incorrect. There is no shame in it and make sure your students know this. Don't pussyfoot around the issue; let them know it is wrong and reassure them that you know that next time they will get it right – you know they will because they are brilliant scholars and learning is a journey.

- Strategy 12: Q & A (p.73) There are many things you can do to ensure students are interacting and following up on the marking and feedback you have provided. When you are marking the piece of work, consider posing some questions to make them think about the learning gaps you have identified and leave space for them to respond to them. This may need training and structuring for students at first so that they know how to best respond to your questions. The questions should make them think about how they could improve. If they do not have the answer, then the necessary resources should be available for the students to find this out at the same time that they receive the feedback.
- Strategy 20: Background knowledge (p.75) It may be that it becomes apparent that in some cases background knowledge is still lacking. If this is the case, then direct the student to resources the next lesson that will help them fill that gap and move forward. Ensure you give them time to gather the information they need and show you that they have done this in some way; for instance write a summary of what they have found out and a plan for how they would incorporate it to improve the piece of work.
- Strategy 21: Think to remember (p.75) You could also pose some problems or tasks for them to ponder and help them consider errors or gaps in learning that are apparent from your marking of their work. You may also choose to set them a follow-up task or rewrite of the original piece (which is covered in the 'Follow-up' phase of the marking and feedback cycle). But, however you choose to address the errors found in their work, make sure that there is some record of the students working on that error so that you can see they have done it and they can look back to ensure they don't make the error again.

Key questions for reflection

1. In this piece of marked work, is it best for your students to be given grades or not?
2. Do you mark work like this regularly? If so, could you create a bank of targets to save you time?
3. Are you sure you are not overloading the student with too much feedback?
4. Does your marking demand high standards from your students at all times?
5. Have you provided feedback that allows them to work on what you are advising them straight away?
6. Are there any clear gaps in background knowledge that are apparent from your marking?

Student approach

Case study

Before Mrs. Casey gives her lovingly-marked work back to the students, she reminds them of the mark scheme that she used and shared with them before they completed the task, so that they are fully aware of what she has marked and how she has approached it. She reiterates the fact that it is always OK to be wrong in their classroom as it is all a part of the learning journey and they are on their way to getting better – we can all improve whatever level we are at. Mrs. Casey takes this opportunity to share some excellent examples from the class' work. Some she names and others she leaves anonymous in line with how the students in questions would react.

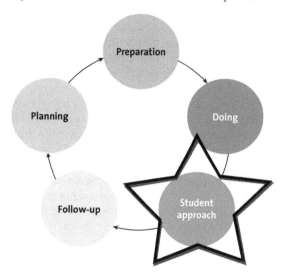

This stage of the marking and feedback cycle looks at how teachers can plan for a culture of positive student response to marking and feedback.

What do you need to think about?

The manner in which students approach the marking and feedback in your lessons can be very telling. It takes time, effort and lots of practice to get a culture of excellence and pride in the work that students produce and an open mind to advice and guidance given in response to it. You create the culture in your classroom when it comes to marking and feedback and how it is received. Even the most challenging class can be trained to appreciate the feedback they get and really begin to progress as a result – it just takes perseverance. The mistake a lot of teachers make is lack of repetition of the teaching of the skills necessary to approach and respond to feedback given. This needs to be repeated and demonstrated multiple times in order for it to be continually effective, even with classes who initially respond well to the process. Don't become complacent with an apparent 'good class' that appears to pick it up quickly; keep pushing them.

Which strategies might you like to use?

- Strategy 5: Student approach (p.68) It is important to build up to giving feedback and marking back to students. Conducting some regular discussions about the purpose of marking and feedback in general and what you expect from the students can be useful. Getting students to understand that marking and feedback is always developmental and should always be approached as such, and to form a professional approach to marking and feedback as part of their job as a student rather than seeing it as a personal attack, is a great life skill they can build with you.

- Strategy 11: High expectations (p.71) Ensuring that students know you will always be honest with them about their work and that you will have nothing but the highest expectations of them because that is what you want for them, makes students feel secure and valued in the long term. Never compromise on the highest expectations for your students or they can begin to distrust your opinion, e.g. if they realise they have not done something well enough and you have said it is fine. Part and parcel of forming strong student–teacher relationships is to ensure that they know you always want the best for them even if that is not what they initially want or feel is necessary. Making them believe you have their backing in everything you do and say is a very important and powerful thing and can really free them up to progress rapidly in their learning.

- Strategy 9: Student mindset (p.69) Building a positive mindset in response to marking and feedback is an essential part of classroom practice for every teacher. If the students see the process as positive and engage with it openly then that is half the battle. Ensuring that your students have a growth mindset whereby they see their own intelligence and knowledge base as living and growing rather than as fixed and static, ensures that they believe that they can improve and that you are a part of that process. All students will be more naturally inclined towards either the fixed or growth mindset so make sure that you are aware of who these students are and take steps towards all students moving towards the growth mindset. Showing them their previous progress, how they have improved and how far they have come can be a great way of opening up the growth mindset to those more inclined towards the fixed mindset.

- Strategy 10: Marking mindset (p.70) Having a well-organised and consistent approach to marking and feedback in student books can help this be clearly visible to students when they look back over their work. They can't argue with the cold, hard facts if they are laid bare in their books. Get some healthy discussion going between your growth mindset and fixed mindset students and explore the outcomes of the discussions as a group. Valuing all the opinions that student bring to the table is important, but ensuring that they have a growth mindset and can appreciate the benefits of such a mindset is important too.

- Strategy 7: Welcome failure (p.68) Helping our students become comfortable with being wrong is a very important lesson that we must guide them through, over and over again. Learning to be comfortable with getting things wrong is so important for us all and students can learn this lesson with you when they receive feedback on their work. Celebrating failure as part of the learning journey and a step closer to perfection is something that can be incorporated in all of our classrooms very easily. Encouraging students to look at the errors that they made in their work first before grades or positive comments, can help them to see what can be done right away to make things even better and aid their progression.

- Strategy 18: Wrong is OK (p.74) Having a clear and consistent approach to feeding back on student errors can really help them to quickly decipher your making and feedback and work towards the next steps smoothly. Clearly highlight where you are making comments and setting targets for improvements that could have been made. Creating a culture where students are hungry for feedback on errors made in their work is what we should be aiming for. To get to a place where students look forward to your feedback on errors, as they know that they can move forward if they take it on board and work on it, is a great aim to have. It is often the case that students will hold back in their work as they fear being wrong and this is a crying shame as they will never reach their full potential if they fear putting themselves out there and taking risks in case they get it wrong. There is nothing wrong with being wrong and we need to get our students to be open to this.

Key questions for reflection

1. Are there some students that always approach your marking negatively? Why do you think this is?
2. Have you modelled how to approach marking and feedback?
3. Have you discussed the point of marking and feedback with your students?
4. Have you established a growth mindset with your class?
5. Have you made it acceptable to be wrong in your classroom?

Follow-up

Case study

Once the students have had time to look at and take in the marking, Mrs. Casey directs them to the follow-up task that she has set. This task ensures that they are

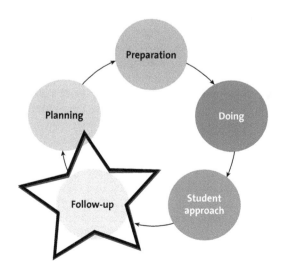

made to look at their targets from the marking and redraft the work with these in mind and make improvements. While the lesson is commencing, Mrs. Casey marks with verbal feedback stampers, making students write down her advice as she says it.

This stage of the marking and feedback cycle explores how teachers can structure the follow-up lessons and ensure that students are getting the most from the marking and feedback that teachers are providing for them.

What do you need to think about?

Once students have been given time and space to read, reflect and take in your marking and feedback, it is important to give them time to take steps in line with your advice and guidance. It is advisable to do this as soon as possible, preferably in the same lesson that they receive the marking and feedback. Providing them with an activity that makes them think about what you have fed back to them, and try to implement any advice, is the best way to get them to progress in their learning and ensure that they are able to take on board all the comments they receive. Getting a routine in place whereby students know what to expect when they get feedback on their work, and can practise getting better at responding to and acting upon it, will mean you don't have to do all the work; they will be able to lead themselves through the process after a while.

Which strategies might you like to use?

- Strategy 21: Think to remember (p.75) When you are setting and undertaking follow-up tasks, ensure you are getting your students to use their brains and really think about what they have done and how they can improve it. Ask them questions rather than just correcting their errors.
- Strategy 12: Q & A (p.73) When asking questions in your marking, question their motives behind choices they have made. Ask if there is another way they could have approached a topic or piece of work. Get them to consider a new element of the task that they did not cover in their work but could have done. Getting them to think and think hard about their work and choices they made is a sure-fire way to get them to remember what it is that they have learnt and how they can move forward. Organise your feedback in their books so that they can clearly answer any questions you have posed for them. This allows you to see that they have taken on board your feedback and also allows them to look back and ensure they are continuing to do what it is that they have committed to in future work they produce.
- Strategy 17: Rework it (p.74) Ensure that the follow-up task that you have set allows them to practise the full range of skills that they were using in the initial task on which you have provided feedback. Asking them to display the same excellence they did in the last task but to also work on the improvements you have highlighted are essential. You can simply ask them to perform the same task once again improving the skills you have highlighted as necessary as they go.

- Strategy 19: Practise everything (p.74) Finding different ways to practise the same skills will really make the learning stick and last in the students' minds. Ensuring that they practise what they are good at as well as what they need to improve upon, will allow them to know what it feels like to use the full range of skills well and not compartmentalise them in to what it feels like to use the skills that they are good with and those that they are not good with.
- Strategy 25: Revise and redraft (p.77) As each skill improves, so too will your students' understanding of how all the skills work together in harmony to form a great piece of work – this is a very satisfying journey for students to go on. Students should expect to have to redo work as standard and understand the benefits of doing this regularly. The lead in this needs to come from you and should be discussed in detail as a class. Looking in detail at their work should be a quiet time of reflection and recognition of their own progress and next steps – it should be a time to relish. Forming this culture is possible and can really allow students the space to flourish.
- Strategy 23: Examples of excellence (p.77) Providing students with examples of excellent finished work for them to compare their own work against during the marking process can be really useful. Crafting their work and the ability to do this well needs to be taught and practised by the students. The more they do it, the better they will become and the more pride and understanding they will have linked to the work they produce. Analysing the work together as a class by looking at how the example of excellence approached the task that was set and discussing its merits can be a real eye-opener for students. You will more than likely have used models with your students in the lessons in the lead up to them completing the piece of work to be marked, but it is very different looking at one once the students have gone through the process of actually creating that piece of work themselves.
- Strategy 26: Public presentation (p.77) Finding the time to celebrate student work often goes by the wayside in the busy school day, but it is so important. Celebration of excellence in your school and own classroom builds in students a sense of security, a tendency to take risks in their work, a confidence in their own abilities and an appreciation of one another's talents. Once a piece of work has been marked, fed back upon and possibly reworked once again is a great time to show off examples of excellence from students in the class. This can take the form of simply showing a model to the class that is taken from a particular student who has done well in the task set – you could remove the name if they are the type to become uncomfortable with the focus being on them; that way they are celebrated but not embarrassed. You could form a display of excellent work with your marking and feedback clearly shown so that students and you can refer back to it at any time in the future. You could ask students to stand and share what you have highlighted them as doing well with in your marking and feedback and explain how and why they did this in their work. Having examples of excellence from a professional source as well

as your own students can open students up to the fact that they can achieve the very best; it is attainable.

Key questions for reflection

1. Have you provided feedback that will allow students to understand how to get better?
2. Have you designed a task that will allow them to work on your feedback and make improvements?
3. Have you shared with your students examples of excellent responses to marking and feedback so that they know what they are aiming for?
4. Have you celebrated the successes that you saw when marking their work?

Planning

Case study

Once she takes the books in and sees what they have produced, Mrs. Casey uses this to help her plan the subsequent lessons. She looks for gaps in skills and knowledge and ensures that she addresses them in the upcoming lessons.

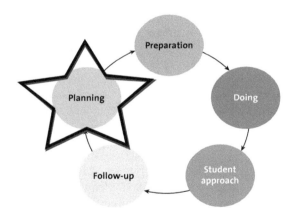

This stage of the marking and feedback cycle considers how planning fits into the process and how teachers can best use the marking and feedback to ensure planning is centred on enabling the students to progress rapidly.

What do you need to think about?

Marking is planning. This is a mantra to live by. The marking and feedback that you undertake should feed directly back into the lesson you are planning for that group of students. It is all well and good having a termly plan and ploughing through it to ensure that you cover everything you should, but have the students really learnt everything that you have diligently taught? If not, then what was the point in covering it? Ensuring that they actually understand concepts and key knowledge that they need in your lessons is essential for progress with all students. If you are not forming or reworking your planning as you go, then you are absolutely going to leave some students behind throughout the term and it is very difficult to get them back once you reach the end of a term or a unit.

Which strategies might you use?

- Strategy 8: Student-teacher feedback (p.68) Ensure that your students' work and the marking you conduct informs your planning at regular intervals. Students are telling you what they have gained in your lesson through their work, so make sure you are listening!
- Strategy 15: Eyes on the prize (p.73) Plan backwards. When you are forming your plan for the year, term, week or lesson always plan backwards keeping the final goal in mind and forming all tasks around the students achieving that goal. If you do this, then it ensures that there is no wasted time in lessons. Every task should have purpose and build towards what you want them to be achieving by the end of the lesson or unit.
- Strategy 20: Background knowledge (p.75) Using previously marked work to see where they are in terms of skills and knowledge can help you build these activities and differentiate for individual students effectively. If it has become glaringly obvious while marking that some or all students are missing a key piece of knowledge in order to use their skill effectively in the tasks, then this again needs to feed straight back in to your planning for the next lesson or week so that that gap is filled and students are able to progress unhindered by this handicap.
- Strategy 16: Chunk it up (p.74) When you are planning lessons, ensure that any skills you are covering are broken down adequately. It is a common mistake to throw too much at students all at once.
- Strategy 28: Repeat and weave (p.79) It is much better to ensure that you plan to break each skill down and take the time to explain things well, check students have understood your explanation and then repeat the process in a different context to ensure it is embedded.
- Strategy 19: Practise everything (p.74) Building in the practice of all skills covered throughout the unit of learning, both in response to observations you have made during marking and feedback but also as standard, is good practice and will allow students to build their skills and knowledge while also embedding those they already have.
- Strategy 25: Revise and redraft (p.77) Plan sessions to do the same or similar work in the future to show both you and the students themselves the progress that they have made.
- Strategy 27: Mix it up (p.78) A good approach is to plan different tasks that cover the same skills and knowledge into the unit of work so that both you and the students are aware of the strengths and gaps that need filling as you go

rather than just at the end of the unit. This makes for a much more confident and well-rounded student.

- Strategy 22: Make it matter (p.77) Making students care about the work they are producing so that they therefore do that work better is vital. There are many ways you can plan to make work matter to students, such as forming a well-valued marking and feedback system where they understand that their work matters to you, or linking the task to their interests or the world around them or sharing with students how the skills and knowledge they are gaining through the task can be used once they are older and in the real world of work. All of these approaches should be planned into your general practice and spread across the units of work through the year. The repetition of these activities and approaches has a cumulative effect and students will eventually be able to see the value in the work themselves without your prompting. It just takes training.
- Strategy 23: Examples of excellence (p.77) It can also help to make work matter to students if you display excellent examples of their work regularly in the classroom and around school, and share and analyse examples of excellence from professional sources as well as past and present students.

Key questions for reflection
1. Does your marking influence your planning and do you reflect on your marking when you are planning future lessons?
2. When you are setting your long-term plans do you identify assessment opportunities and activities that all lead to your goal for the students?

Summary

Making your marking cyclical like this will ensure that progress is ongoing regardless of the skill or piece of knowledge being taught at any one time. Everything is interlinked and flows nicely if this style of approach is followed – students and teacher work in tandem and the smooth motion of the learning is easy for all to follow while still being challenging.

Preparing your students for assessed work is not only of benefit to you as a teacher, in terms of having better quality work to mark, but is also hugely empowering to pupils as they are given control of their own progress. They are given the right tools to do well and they have ownership. Taking the time to mark the students' work produced after this will be a much more pleasurable experience as the work will have a core of knowledge, skill, pride and effort. Enabling your students to work with your marking and feedback well is a real life skill. Being able to take advice, work on it and see immediate improvement is a powerful experience. Giving students meaningful tasks to show they understand your feedback is essential and will compound the learning that has taken place because of receiving the marking.

Chapter 5 takeaway

Teaching tip

Get a routine in place

Having a regular and predictable routine in place for marking and feedback will allow your students to learn how best to respond to the feedback they receive as they have chances to practise over and over again. If they are constantly having to relearn how you are approaching marking and feedback then that is what they will focus on, not the actual feedback itself.

Pass it on

Sharing your ideas – Twitter

Twitter is a great place to share good practice. On Twitter you have 140 characters to share what you will with the world. Some refer to it as 'micro-blogging'. You can set your account to be 'private' so that no one can see your tweets unless you approve them whilst still being able to see the tweets of those that you follow unhindered, or you can have an 'open' account that everyone can see. Twitter can be, and often is, used for mundane purposes that are very far from sharing of good practice. But behind the inane wittering, lies an underbelly of dedicated and interesting folk who are sharing and discussing teaching and learning in an open and honest manner – this is well worth checking out. Following well-known teachers and educational bodies on Twitter will get you off to a good start, as this will fill your timeline with interesting and useful tweets on teaching and learning.

By using the appropriate hashtag, you will be sharing your ideas, experiences and tips with a specific audience with a specific interest in what you are talking about. For instance, by including #UKEdChat in your tweet, you will ensure that others in the UK who are interested in education can find your tweet even if they do not search for or follow you specifically. You could use Twitter to share specific experiences you have undertaken in your classroom in your marking and feedback journey. You could ask fellow educational professionals for advice or guidance on a marking and feedback issue you are tackling. You could share an interesting marking and feedback article or blog you have come across or written. You could link up with others who are interested in marking and feedback and set up a long distance marking and feedback project. Give it a go.

Colleague catch-up

Have a conversation with a colleague about whether they have any routines they follow when it comes to their marking and feedback. Talk to colleagues about your own ideas and listen to their views. Speak to teachers in different subjects or key stages for interest. What are the differences and similarities in your viewpoints?

Share and tweet

Share how you have been using the marking and feedback cycle and what has worked or not worked for you on Twitter using the hashtag #BloomsCPD.

CPD book club recommendation

Doug Lemov – *Teach Like a Champion*
(See Bibliography and further reading, page 295)

Bloggers' corner

Alex Quigley has some decent posts on marking and feedback that are well worth a read. Visit his blog at http://www.huntingenglish.com.

TO DO LIST:

- ☐ Get a marking and feedback routine in place in your classroom
- ☐ Tweet how you have been using the marking and feedback cycle and what has worked or not worked for you and check out what others have said by using the hashtag #BloomsCPD
- ☐ Talk with colleagues about marking and feedback routines that they have in their classroom
- ☐ Check out Alex Quigley's blog posts on marking and feedback: http://www.huntingenglish.com
- ☐ Read *Teach Like a Champion* by Doug Lemov

6 Evaluating progress

So now you have the marking cycle in its entirety clearly buzzing around your mind and hopefully you have started to put the new strategies into practice!

As you integrate the new strategies, make sure that you have thought through all the possible pitfalls and nuances that are necessary to make it work with your students in your classroom. In this chapter, we explore the reflection questions that were posed for each stage of the marking and feedback cycle in the last chapter in a little more detail. This should be the starting point of your thinking process for each stage of the cycle – only you know what you need to focus on and take into consideration when it comes to your marking and feedback. Make sure you have done the thinking so that you can make it successful in your setting.

Evaluating the key questions for reflection from the marking and feedback cycle

Preparation

1. Do you currently give students the tools they need in order to succeed in tasks you set?

Are your students really clear about what you expect of them in the task you have set that will be assessed? You need to make a judgment call as to what they need in order to have the best chance to succeed. If your students lose out on marks because they didn't understand what you wanted from them, then that is unfair. You have a duty to ensure that they are set up for success and not failure.

How can you check what is working well in this area?

Well, there are many ways...

- Consider completing an audit of pre-assessment lessons in your schemes of work.
- Have you provided time for them to read, annotate, discuss and understand the mark scheme?
- Have you planned in time to show them how you mark their work so they fully understand the process you will undertake with their finished work?
- Get students to mark their work using the mark scheme you went through with them and then mark their marking so you can see how much they understood about what they were being assessed on.

2. Do you make the work that will be marked matter to your students?

When you set up a task, do you make your students care about what they are creating? When students feel that they have a vested interest in the work that they are creating, then they are much more likely to put effort into it. It may be that all you need to do is link the task to the real world around you and take it outside the classroom, the exercise book and the resource you are using. Showing news clips, sharing real life stories or linking it to the local area are all great approaches. Play to your students' interests and hobbies outside of the classroom; knowing your students is essential to get this right.

How can you check what is working well in this area?

- Set up a display board in your classroom and keep the work displayed regularly updated.
- Let students know when new work is going to be placed up so that they can check in on the board regularly.
- Keep an eye on who comes to check you board and how often. It may surprise you.

3. Do you feel you explain tasks that will be marked well enough?

Do you ever look at the responses that you receive from a set task, realise that they are all making the same errors and consider whether you actually made a mistake in your approach to explaining the task? If a task is explained badly it can really have a negative impact on what the students produce. Students are looking to you and your explanation in order to produce their work correctly and to a high standard. If your explanation is low standard then so too will their work be.

How can you check what is working well in this area?

- One great way to check how well you have explained things is to ask students at random, and without warning, to repeat back what you have asked them to do. You could even ask different students to repeat back different bits of the instruction to you just to keep them on their toes.
- Ask students to explain the task in their own words to someone next to them. This makes them think through what you have said and also check for errors with a peer. Then select another student at random and see if there are still errors in understanding of the task.
- Another sure-fire way to know that you have explained something badly is if all, or a lot, of your students have made the same error. More than likely this is your error in explanation.
- You could be brave and film yourself explaining various tasks and watch the footage back to see what it is like from the watchers'/listeners' perspective.
- You could even ask fellow teachers to give you objective feedback on how you explain tasks either from filmed footage or live in lessons.

4. Do you show students examples of excellence so they know what they are aiming for?

Showing students examples of excellence prior to starting work ensures that they have access to and knowledge of what the gold standard is in this subject area. You do not want them copying the content, however, or for it to have the effect of blocking any original ideas they may come up with as the content of the example is consuming their thoughts. Therefore, it is a good idea to show an example that has a slightly different focus but the same approach or style to the one you want your students to produce. That way they get an insight into what you are looking for while not being given the direct answer. Your examples can come from other students, the media or textbooks; it does not matter as long as it is showing the top level of what you are looking for. Discussing and breaking down what is going in to the finished piece is essential for students to be able to replicate the skill behind the work themselves. You could also craft a live example of the section of the type of work you are looking for from the students on the interactive whiteboard, talking through your decisions and thought processes as you go. There is something quite special for students to see a teacher create the same type of work that they are expected to do live in the classroom for all to see.

How can you check what is working well in this area?

- Very simple really – look to see whether your students have started to emulate the style of the examples of excellence more often.
- Look for things that you have highlighted as good practice in the examples in your students work. Celebrate when these have been used well to continue to the striving for success.

5. Do you give your students chances to practise the skills needed in the assessed work?

Finding different ways to practise the skills needed to do well in the work you are assessing can be really fun. Mix it up a bit and find new ways of practising the skills they need for your subject area and the assessment in particular and get practising. Make sure you make it overt to the students the skills they are using and how that skill crosses over into their work. Perfect practice makes students perform better and quickly, so these skills need to be visited and revisited regularly.

How can you check what is working well in this area?

- A student survey could come into play to test this area of your practice as you develop.
- Try devising a questionnaire or simple test that specifically assesses the skills you are using with the students and giving it to them at the start and at the end of a teaching unit or few lessons, comparing the results.

6. Do your preparation tasks make students think deeply about the work they are producing?

Are you working out the grey matter of your students hard enough to make your lessons memorable? It is well-known that the more deeply you are made to think, the more the learning will stick. Asking questions and provoking thought through interesting statements around the topic can really get your students thinking deeply.

How can you check what is working well in this area?

- Ask students to recall and tell you about activities in which you have not used deep thinking activities, and also ones where you have purposefully designed and used deep thinking activities – see if they remember one more readily than the other. You may well be surprised.

Marking and feedback

1. In this piece of marked work, is it best for your students to be given grades or not?

Whether or not you give grades to individual pieces of work is a highly debated topic and has been for some time. Some believe that it is important to give feedback in terms of grades to students for individual work because the transparency allows students to see exactly where they are in a piece of work and progress more quickly. Others feel that as soon as a student sees a grade or mark that they switch off and take no heed of the feedback given to them to progress onwards and upwards. Both approaches can be useful and should be experimented with in your subject area, year group and classroom to see what suits your students.

How can you check what is working well in this area?

- Set an assessed task which you grade in the traditional way and which the students then rework with the feedback in mind. Then set an assessed task for which you give only feedback but no mark and then ask them to rework the work with the feedback in mind.
- Have a look at the data for both sets of tests and see which your students perform better in. Maybe some groups are better with grades and others without?
- This is a very interesting data task to undertake. Which method allowed the most progress in your class?

2. Do you mark work like this regularly? If so, could you create a bank of targets to save you time?

Having a bank of targets that you use all the time when marking work is really helpful in terms of saving you time and also allowing you to spend more time actually marking and assessing the work your students produce. Using the mark scheme to create a bank of levelled targets can be a really helpful tool that can be used again and again. Also, as other teachers in your subject will also need these, you could share out the work in creating these targets and save even more time. Everyone needs them so why not help one another out. The students could then be provided with the targets and each one given a number so that you can just pop the number in the margin at the bottom of the work for the students to then copy out the targets. This gives you the assurance that students have made that first contact with your marking and have actually read what you have asked them to do.

How can you check what is working well in this area?

- Take note of the time it takes you to mark work now you are using a target bank. Guaranteed it will be a lot less time for each batch of marking.
- Using the same wording for targets you are using with your students should make it a lot easier for your students to access what you are asking them to do, as once they are familiar with the language of your targets they have already done some of the thinking, before even coming to your feedback as time goes on.
- Take note of how much more easily your students can talk about your feedback and given targets as opposed to before using target banks.

3. Are you sure you are not overloading the student with too much feedback?

Making sure that you give students feedback that is not too overwhelming is vital. If we are putting students off by the sheer amount of feedback we have provided, then we are shooting ourselves in the foot and wasting our time. Decide what will make a difference and actually make the students' work better if they were to use the same approach in a similar piece of work next time. Baby steps are by far the best approach when it comes to giving feedback.

How can you check what is working well in this area?

- You could take the opportunity to conduct a book scrutiny to review this area of your practice. Collect in the class set of books and just look at your feedback in isolation. How many sentences have you used on average? How many targets have you given each piece of work on average? Is there any evidence of providing too much feedback and what did you do that for; what kind of task?
- Think carefully about how your students would approach the feedback you have provided. How can you make it better? What target can you give yourself about making your marking more accessible and useful for students?
- You could also ask students to tell you what you have given them as targets at random and ask them not to look at their books. If they can't tell you, then they either have not read it or there may well be too much there for them to really remember and work on.

4. Does your marking demand high standards from your students at all times?

Having high standards all the time makes your students feel secure and know exactly where they stand and what to expect from you. If you allow some things to slip, they will get the message that you do not care and they should not care either – not ever a place you want to be with your students.

How can you check what is working well in this area?

- One approach you could take to look at this element of your practice is a marking analysis. You could take as the focus a consideration of your wording and what you point out in your marking and make sure that you are happy with the message you are sending to your students.

- Tone of voice and emphasis cannot be conveyed in your written feedback so it is vital that it is clear that you expect the very best from them.

5. Have you provided feedback that allows them to work on what you are advising them straight away?

Allowing time after each piece of marked work to really get the students thinking about your feedback by completing a task to improve their original is so important. Putting advice into action quickly really does compound the learning that the students undergo when they focus on and take on board your feedback. It can be tempting to skip this phase with all the many things we need to get through in school now, but resist the temptation to do this! It is important and will allow your students to do better than if they merrily skip onwards to the next task; there is much less likelihood of them repeating errors or staying at the same level if you allow the time to act upon your feedback.

How can you check what is working well in this area?

- Consider doing a review of your schemes of work or long-term plans. What tasks have you set directly following assessed work being given back? Does that work test the skills they need to work on?
- If you are confident that you have designed your long-term plans with the follow-up tasks carefully crafted to allow for further progress, then you could conduct a review of the tasks the students actually undertake in the form of a book scrutiny. Look at the actual student responses following task setting after feedback from assessed work. Have the tasks done what you intended them to do? Have the tasks had impact or would you redesign them slightly in future?

6. Are there any clear gaps in background knowledge that are apparent from your marking?

Knowing your students and what they are bringing to the table when you teach them is not an easy thing to achieve, but it is essential in order to pitch lessons correctly and get the most from your students. Powering on through a unit of work and not checking the knowledge your students already have can be hugely detrimental to the speed of the student learning and their progress. Holes in knowledge can cause misconceptions and students becoming massively confused. Get the lay of the land in your classroom before you jump ahead.

How can you check what is working well in this area?

- A review of supporting resources available in your classroom may be of use here. Do you have appropriate and accessible help sheets, books and recommended websites that the students could quite easily use if they have obvious gaps in background knowledge on a certain area you are covering in class? If not, then invest in getting the right things in your classroom as a time-saver to address one-off individual needs as and when they pop up. You can direct them directly to your resources through your marking and feedback.

- You could also conduct a review of your planning documents, long-term plans and schemes of work. Looking over your plans and ensuring that you have highlighted essential knowledge that the students would need in order to access your lesson, and checking that this knowledge is secure as you go through the term, can save you a lot of time later on.
- Filling the gaps as you go rather than at the end is a better approach than loading them up at the end of a unit when the learning has been covered.

Student review

1. Are there some students that always approach your marking negatively? Why do you think this is?

Students do not all naturally find it easy to connect with and act upon marking and feedback they are given in school. They need to be trained and nudged along in order to get them to where we need them to be. If students are approaching your marking or feedback negatively, then they will be gaining much less from the process than others.

How can you check what is working well in this area?

- Form an action plan to get these students back in line with the attitude you want to foster in your classroom in terms of marking and feedback. This may take time but it is time well spent.
- Monitor the students and how they respond to the marking and feedback as you progress through the plan. You could try more peer discussions on marking and feedback; pairing them up with more positive students.
- You could try different approaches to marking and feedback such as giving them oral feedback more often that they write down, or using codes so that they can write out the feedback themselves.

2. Have you modelled how to approach marking and feedback?

Making sure that your students know what excellent marking looks like and what goes into it, is much more complex than just exposing them to it through your marking, although this is an important part of the process. Live marking and regular discussions around marking decisions or approaches are essential to allow students to understand and become confident in the reading of and acting upon marking and feedback. Never presume they understand. Repetition and revising is key in order to achieve mastery.

How can you check what is working well in this area?

- Ask a colleague in your subject area or key stage to buddy up with you and both practise your modelling of various tasks you are due to feed back on in the coming term and advise one another on how you can best improve. Two heads are most definitely better than one.

- The best tester in terms of the success you are having in this area is the students' feedback to one another. Are they picking up the good habits you have shown and explained to them when they are feeding back to one another?

3. Have you discussed the point of marking and feedback with your students?

Sometimes we forget that students have not chosen a career as a teacher, or been trained to become one, and presume that they understand the point of what we are doing when we are marking and feeding back to them. They need careful training and open discussions about why we do the wild and wonderful things we do when we mark their work. Where have we got the targets from? What will happen if they achieve the target you have given them? How does this marking and feedback link to other marking and feedback they may have had from you? They will have many questions in their mind even if they don't realise it. By openly exploring the marking and feedback process and the point of it all, you will bring students along with you. Make sure you take the mystery out of the process.

How can you check what is working well in this area?

- Once you have held the open discussions you can create a space in your lesson for a questions and answer session. Give work back to students and ask them to reflect on why you have said the things you have said in your marking and feedback.
- Do this regularly and it will soon become second nature to them and you. They will all understand the process of marking and feeding back and that is beneficial for all.

4. Have you established a growth mindset with your class?

Developing students' confidence in their own ability to improve can be a real challenge in some cases. Students who believe that they are not intelligent will not be able to push themselves to improve very easily. It is absolutely a part of our job to ensure that we build a student's confidence in his or her own abilities. We need to find ways to help them see that they can improve if they want to and realise the great sense of achievement that comes with that.

How can you check what is working well in this area?

- You will be able to see when this is working well as students will approach your marking and feedback in a positive and open manner rather than with apathy or defensive comments.
- Things you can do to encourage this is emphasise that being wrong is OK.
- Speak to your class passionately and from the heart about what students do well in your classroom; taking careful consideration of celebrating all students and what they bring to the table in terms of skill and effort. Make them and their work feel appreciated.

- Your marking and feedback should be honest and developmental but also uplifting and assuring of students' abilities; monitor it carefully through regular auditing of students' books whom you know are more inclined towards a fixed mindset.

5. Have you made it acceptable to be wrong in your classroom?

Making it OK to be wrong in your classroom is incredibly powerful. Celebrate errors and applaud students for taking the risk and putting themselves out there. Share with the class that these students, the ones who are not scared of being wrong, have the ability to go further and learn more quickly than those students who play it safe and never want to be wrong.

How can you check what is working well in this area?

- When students are happy to receive feedback pointing out their errors and even relish it, you know you are moving forward in this area.
- Watch your students carefully when they receive feedback that points out errors and see if you can see a change over time with your re-education of their views on being wrong.
- Try going a step further and asking students to let a peer-marking buddy see their feedback first and share where they have gone wrong and what steps are needed to improve verbally before they are allowed to look at their own work. If students are OK with this process you have really done well!

Follow-up

1. Have you provided feedback that will allow students to understand how to get better?

Feedback done well is easily understood while still being challenging and making a difference to student progress and understanding of a skill or topic. Making sure that your marking and feedback is clear and actionable is vital to students' ability to move confidently and consciously towards self-improvement and rapid progress in your subject area.

How can you check what is working well in this area?

- Conduct an audit of your marking and ensure that your feedback is specific and actionable by the students. Anything too vague or that they are unable to work on straight away may be a step too far.
- Once marking and feedback has been given and the students have had time to take it in, ask them to tell you what their next steps are orally. Go around the class and ask each student to tell you out loud what they are specifically doing in the follow-up task to improve their work even more.

2. Have you designed a task that will allow students to work on your feedback and make improvements?

The choice of follow-up task can really make or break your marking and feedback cycle. The right task that allows students to very overtly work on the targets you have given them while still reviewing what they did before is essential. The wrong task can really scupper any plans you or the student may have of progress and improvement. Think very carefully about what you want them to do as a follow-up task. It is tempting to ask them to do the task again every time but with improvements you have suggested. Now while this is a fine task to do from time to time, it can become very dull and take up quite a lot of time. Try to think of ways they can practise the skill without becoming bored of the task and it losing impact.

How can you check what is working well in this area?

- You could team up with colleagues and design a bank of reasonably short and simple tasks that allow students to practise particular skills in your subject area. Divide out the tasks and create some simple reusable resources that everyone can benefit from.
- You could use these simple short tasks as the follow-up task directly after the marking and feedback and then just interweave the skills in again and again more subtly over the next few lessons to really embed the skill.
- Student progress in the skills necessary in your subject is how you will see impact and what is working. Make sure you review this on your own as well as a team if you have rallied together to create the resources.

3. Have you shared with your students examples of excellent responses to marking and feedback so that they know what they are aiming for?

You will have already shown examples of excellence for the original task but don't think your job is done there. You need to model what a good response to feedback will look like too, remember. Showing the students how they can be good at improving is just as important as them being clear about what the original task is all about through a model.

How can you check what is working well in this area?

- You could model live on the interactive whiteboard how to respond to feedback and play the part of the student for your class to see.
- Depending on the class, you could ask a student to share their work and feedback they have been given and work with them live to start the improvement process with a visualiser, if you have one. It is important to talk through the thought process the student will have to go through too.
- Allowing students to talk to and with you about this process will give you a real insight as to how well this is going in your classroom. Get them discussing

the process once they have been shown it and listen in to their conversations to check for understanding.

4. Have you celebrated the successes that you saw when marking their work?

Publicly celebrating the successes that you have seen in students' work shows a real appreciation of the their efforts and allows them to really see that you have paid careful attention to their work. Often students will look at the marking and not really link you and the written word together. Or, they may only look at the improvements or what they see as negative. Celebrate the positives.

How can you check what is working well in this area?

- Anonymously celebrate what an individual has achieved in the task so that the students look down at their work to see if it is their work you are talking about.
- Consider using a student questionnaire or quiz at the end of the feedback lesson to check how much they remember about what people did well in the task according to your whole-class celebration at the start of the lesson.

Planning

1. Does your marking influence your planning and do you reflect on your marking when you are planning?

Ensuring that you adjust your plans in line with what you discover when you mark your students' books can directly improve your students' outcomes as well as your lessons in general. If you are able to be responsive in your teaching then the students' learning will improve and come with ease.

How can you check what is working well in this area?

- Make sure as you mark a set of books or papers that you keep a note of errors that students are making as you go along, so that this is easy to use and look back at when you come to plan for future lessons or indeed future years or groups where you teach the same topic. Make sure you have this list readily available and use it to form your future planning as you go.
- The way to see if you are moving forward in this area is if your students do not make the same errors as you go through the rest of the unit of learning because you have pre-planned to not allow this to be the case.

2. When you are setting your long-term plans, do you identify assessment opportunities and activities that all lead to your goal for the students?

The structuring and sequencing of your lessons to ensure all skills and knowledge are being covered is the only way you can ensure that all students will be able to access the assessment you plan to mark and feedback on. If this is not done well, then you are unaccountably going to be marking work that is below the actual level your students are at. And this will be your fault! You need to get this part right for your time to be spent well when you come to marking and giving feedback to your students.

How can you check what is working well in this area?

- It is simple really – review your schemes of work and long-term plans and ensure that you have clearly mapped out the assessment opportunities. Review whether the lessons in the lead up to the assessments are appropriate and achieving what you need in order to prepare the student well for their assessment.
- Planning out your lesson objectives for each lesson for the entire unit to ensure you have covered all skills and knowledge needed to be successful in the assessment is a great approach.
- Careful reviewing of plans is a necessity here.

Chapter 6 takeaway

Teaching tip
Sharing is caring
Share what goes on in your classroom and share it often. We teachers can be too coy about the great stuff we do and it needs to be known. There is so much negativity in the press, and in general around teaching, that to spread a little joy and let people know what great work you are doing is you doing your bit to make sure teaching is represented for all it can be; the highs and special moments as well as the tough bits.

Pass it on
Sharing your ideas – Facebook
Facebook is not just for family catch-ups and photos of nights out. You can use it as a professional development tool, but obviously if you have a personal Facebook account you will want to keep this separate. Unlike Twitter, there is no limit to the number of characters you can use in any one post. Again you can set your account to 'private' so only those you choose can see it or 'public' whereby everyone can see you. Facebook is thriving with mini online teaching and learning communities. If you 'like' the right pages and 'follow' the right educational professional accounts then there is a whole other side to Facebook.

You could set up a Facebook group for a marking and feedback project you are doing with colleagues. You could post articles and blogs you find on marking and feedback. You could ask advice of the teaching and learning communities on marking and feedback issues. You could set up a group for students to share their experiences of marking and feedback. You could communicate with parents and carers about marking and feedback and how to decipher it and help their children better. Have a play about with it and see if there is something you find useful.

Students on board

Can you set up any inter-school marking and feedback projects? Perhaps you could arrange to have a teacher in another school get their students to produce the same piece of work and swap over for marking. Or, maybe get the students to create advice leaflets for one another on how best to mark and give feedback to one another and exchange their leaflets.

Share and tweet

Tweet how you are sharing your excellent marking and feedback practice on Twitter using the hashtag #BloomsCPD.

CPD book club recommendation

Ron Berger – *An Ethic of Excellence*
(See Bibliography and further reading, page 295)

Bloggers' corner

Chris Curtis has some interesting posts on marking and feedback that are well worth a read. Visit his blog at http://learningfrommymistakesenglish.blogspot.co.uk.

TO DO LIST:

- ☐ Tweet your approaches to embedding marking practices in your classroom and check out what others have said by using the hashtag #BloomsCPD
- ☐ Check out Chris Curtis' blog posts on marking and feedback: http://learningfrommymistakesenglish.blogspot.co.uk
- ☐ Read *An Ethic of Excellence* by Ron Berger

7 Self-evaluation and reflection

Hopefully your reading so far has prompted and supported you in exploring and improving your marking and feedback practice. Now is the time to think about what steps you have taken so far and what you would like to accomplish in the near and far future in your marking and feedback. If you feel that you are no further along than when you started reading, then I suggest completing some of the 'To do' lists at the end of each of the previous chapters before continuing to complete the next questionnaire in this chapter. It really is important for you to have attempted to apply some thinking and action to your marking and feedback practice before moving on to the questionnaire, so that you can have fully benefited from the processes outlined in the book.

How and why to complete the questionnaire

In order to keep progressing in your marking and feedback it is vital that you reflect on your progress so far. Often teachers I have worked with have said to me at this point, 'But I know what I've done and what I'm strong and weak in.' However, without dedicated reflection time it is very rare that this is truly the case. Quiet, focused time given over to real reflection brings up things that you might not even realise were there. It is always time well spent. The important thing is to note down your reflections and findings and make a plan of action going forward as a result of your musings.

You will remember the questionnaire process from Chapter 2 (page 11), but here is a reminder.

Quick response approach

If your preference for the self-evaluation is to go with your gut only, then simply fill in the quick response section after each question with the first thing that comes in to your mind when you ask yourself the question. Do not mull over the question too carefully, simply read thoroughly and answer quickly. This approach will give you an overview of your current understanding and practice in marking and feedback and will take relatively little time. Just make sure you are uninterrupted, in a quiet place and able to complete the questionnaire in one sitting with no distractions so that you get focused and honest answers.

Considered response approach

If you choose to take a more reflective and detailed approach, then you can leave the quick response section blank and go straight on to reading the further guidance section under each question. This guidance provides prompt questions and ideas to get you thinking in detail about the question being answered and is designed to open up a wider scope in your answer. It will also enable you to look at your experience and pull examples into your answer to back up your statements. You may want to complete a few questions at a time and take breaks, or you may be prepared to sit and work through the questions all in one sitting to ensure you remain focused. This approach does take longer, but it can lead to a more in-depth understanding of your current marking and feedback practice, and you will gain more from the process than the quick response alone.

Combined approach

A thorough approach, and one I recommend, would be to use both approaches together regardless of personal preference. There is clear value in both approaches being used together. This would involve you firstly answering the self-evaluation quick response questions by briefly noting down your instinctual answers for all questions. The next step would be to return to the start of the self-evaluation, read the further guidance and then answer the questions once more, slowly and in detail forming more of a narrative around each question and pulling in examples from your own experience. Following this you would need to read over both responses and form a comprehensive and honest summary in your mind of your answers and a final view of where you feel you stand right now in your marking and feedback practice.

• I have done this self-evaluation before. • I only want a surface level overview of my current understanding and practice. • I work better when I work at speed. • I don't have much time.	**Quick**

• I have never done this self-evaluation before. • I want a deeper understanding of my current understanding and practice. • I work better when I take my time and really think things over. • I have some time to do this self-evaluation.	**Considered**

• I have never done this self-evaluation before. • I have done this self-evaluation before. • I want a comprehensive and full understanding of my current understanding and practice and want to compare that to what I thought before taking the self-evaluation. • I have a decent amount of time to dedicate to completing this self-evaluation.	**Combined**

Fig. 4 How should I approach the self-evaluation questionnaire?

This is the longest of the three approaches to this questionnaire but will give you a comprehensive and full understanding of your current practice, thoughts and feelings in relation to marking and feedback. You will be surprised at the difference you see between the quick response and the considered response answers to the same questions. It can be very illuminating.

Rate yourself

The final part of the self-evaluation is to rate yourself. This section will ask you to rate your confidence and happiness in each area that has been covered in the questionnaire with a view to working on these areas for improvement. The table below shows how the scale works: the higher the number you allocate yourself, the better you feel you are performing in that area.

Rating	Definition
1	Not at all. I don't. None at all. Not happy. Not confident at all.
2	Rarely. Barely. Very little. Very unconfident.
3	Not often at all. Not much. Quite unconfident.
4	Not particularly. Not really. Not a lot. Mildly unconfident.
5	Neutral. Unsure. Don't know. Indifferent.
6	Sometimes. At times. Moderately. A little bit. Mildly confident.
7	Quite often. A fair bit. Some. A little confident.
8	Most of the time. More often than not. Quite a lot. Quite confident.
9	The majority of the time. A lot. Very confident.
10	Completely. Very much so. A huge amount. Extremely happy. Extremely confident.

Fig. 5 Rate yourself scale definitions

Marking and feedback reflection questionnaire

QUESTION 1: What new things have you considered or tried that you have liked in terms of marking and feedback?

Quick response:

_____

_____

_____

_____

Questions for consideration

- Are there any new areas of marking and feedback you have tried in the classroom that have brought you pleasure?
- Have you formed any new routines in or out of the classroom in your marking and feedback and if so, how have they gone?
- How have your students reacted to changes you have made and new things you have tried? What did they like?

Considered response:

_____

_____

_____

_____

_____

_____

_____

Rate yourself

QUESTION 1: How happy are you that you have tried all you wanted to try in your marking and feedback so far?

1   2   3   4   5   6   7   8   9   10

QUESTION 2: What changes have you made in your marking and feedback practice that you feel have had an impact upon student attainment and achievement in your classroom?

Quick response:

_____

_____

_____

_____

Questions for consideration

- Have you seen an impact on attainment and achievement as a result of any of the changes you have made or techniques you have implemented?
- When you have seen a positive impact, what had you done differently?
- Have you noticed whether students are more engaged with your marking and feedback?
- Have you had success with peer- and self-marking and feedback?
- What have you tried that did not have a positive impact on student attainment and achievement? Would you try the same approach again but do it differently?
- Have you seen an impact on attainment and achievement for any particular group or age of student that perhaps you had not previously? Why is this?

Considered response:

_____

_____

_____

_____

Rate yourself

QUESTION 2: How much impact on student achievement and attainment do you feel your marking and feedback has now that you have made changes to your practice?

1   2   3   4   5   6   7   8   9   10

QUESTION 3: How would you now describe your general approach to marking and feedback and how has it changed?

Quick response:

_____

_____

_____

Questions for consideration

- How has your everyday marking and feedback practice changed?
- Do you mix up the marking and feedback approaches you use more or less than before?
- Have you become more or less routined in your marking and feedback and why?
- Do you work more or less at home than before?
- Do you find yourself more or less behind with marking than before?

Considered response:

_____

_____

_____

_____

_____

_____

_____

_____

_____

_____

Rate yourself

QUESTION 3: How happy are you with your approach to marking and feedback at the moment?

1   2   3   4   5   6   7   8   9   10

QUESTION 4: What educational theories, research, ideas or case studies do you now have an interest in and how does it inform and influence your practice?

Quick response:

_____

_____

_____

_____

Questions for consideration

- Which piece of educational research, theory or idea explored in this book or found independently has influenced your marking and feedback practices or thinking, if any?
- Do you feel more or less inclined to look into educational research, studies, and theories on marking and feedback?
- Have you discussed research or case studies on marking and feedback with any colleagues?
- Have you conducted any research into marking and feedback yourself or as part of a team within your school setting?
- How do you feel teachers or schools as a whole should use the findings of educational research on marking and feedback?

Considered response:

_____

_____

_____

_____

_____

_____

Rate yourself

QUESTION 4: How confident are you with your knowledge of educational research into marking and feedback?

1	2	3	4	5	6	7	8	9	10

QUESTION 5: What have you shared or discussed regarding marking and feedback with colleagues outside your department?

Quick response:

_____

_____

_____

_____

Questions for consideration

- Have you shared any of your marking and feedback experiences with staff across the whole school?
- Have you sought out discussions with staff in other departments or teaching years to your own?

Considered response:

_____

_____

_____

_____

_____

_____

_____

_____

_____

_____

_____

_____

Rate yourself

QUESTION 5: How confident are you about sharing your ideas with others on a whole-school level?

1   2   3   4   5   6   7   8   9   10

QUESTION 6: What have you shared or discussed regarding marking and feedback with colleagues in your department?

Quick response:

_____

_____

_____

_____

Questions for consideration

- Have you shared your marking and feedback experiences with your department?
- Have you sought out marking and feedback discussions with staff in your department?
- Have you worked with another member of your department on a marking and feedback project of any sort?
- Has anything changed in your department as a result of discussion or project work on marking and feedback with a colleague in your department?
- Have you influenced how marking and feedback is approached in your department through your discussions, suggestions or actions?
- Have any of your previous opposing views to your departmental policy on marking and feedback now aligned? If so why?

Considered response:

_____

_____

_____

_____

_____

_____

_____

Rate yourself

QUESTION 6: How confident are you about sharing your ideas with others on a departmental level?

| 1 | 2 | 3 | 4 | 5 | 6 | 7 | 8 | 9 | 10 |

QUESTION 7: Where do you feel your strengths now lie in marking and feedback?

Quick response:

_____

_____

_____

_____

Questions for consideration

- What would you now consider your strengths in terms of marking and feedback?
- Have these strengths changed since completing the last self-evaluation?
- Are there any elements of your marking and feedback that you have been praised for either by in-school monitoring, colleagues, students or parents since the last self-evaluation

Considered response:

_____

_____

_____

_____

_____

_____

_____

_____

_____

_____

_____

Rate yourself

QUESTION 7: How confident do are when it comes to your marking and feedback practice?

1	2	3	4	5	6	7	8	9	10

QUESTION 8: Where do you feel your weaknesses now lie in marking and feedback?

Quick response:

_____

_____

_____

_____

Questions for consideration

- What would you now consider are your areas for improvement in terms of marking and feedback?
- Have these areas for improvement changed since the last self-evaluation?
- Are there any weak elements of your marking and feedback that have been mentioned or highlighted to you either by in-school monitoring, colleagues, students or parents since the last self-evaluation?
- Have you been offered any help or training for these weaknesses in marking and feedback?
- Have you undertaken any training in or reading about your weak marking and feedback areas in your own time?

Considered response:

_____

_____

_____

_____

_____

_____

_____

_____

Rate yourself

QUESTION 8:How serious do you feel your weaknesses are when it comes to marking and feedback?

1	2	3	4	5	6	7	8	9	10

QUESTION 9: What would you like to try in your marking and feedback practices that you have not already tried?

Quick response:

_____

_____

_____

_____

Questions for consideration

- Since the last self-evaluation, have you spotted a gap in your marking and feedback practices that you feel needs filling? What approach have you considered to fill this gap?
- Is there an approach to marking and feedback that you have read and liked in this book that you have not yet tried in your own classroom?
- What has stopped you trying it thus far?
- What is the next thing you would like to trial in your marking and feedback practices? How do you plan to go about it?

Considered response:

_____

_____

_____

_____

_____

_____

_____

_____

_____

Rate yourself

QUESTION 9: How confident do you feel when it comes to trying something new with marking and feedback?

1	2	3	4	5	6	7	8	9	10

QUESTION 10: Is there anything that is holding you back in developing your marking and feedback?

Quick response:

_____

_____

_____

_____

Questions for consideration

- What area of your marking and feedback do you really want to improve upon?
- What training do you feel you are lacking in your marking and feedback?
- Have you tried to overcome any marking and feedback hurdles that you face in your school or classroom? If so how did it go?

Considered response:

_____

_____

_____

_____

_____

_____

_____

_____

_____

_____

_____

_____

Rate yourself

QUESTION 10: How much do you feel you are being held back in terms of improving your marking and feedback?

1   2   3   4   5   6   7   8   9   10

QUESTION 11: Is there anything that you have tried in your marking and feedback as a result of reading this book so far?

Quick response:

_____

_____

_____

_____

Questions for consideration

- Have you discussed any theories or ideas explored in this book with any colleagues?
- What level of self-evaluation did you complete at the start of the book? Was it helpful?
- Have you tried any new marking and feedback practices discussed in this book? Were they helpful?
- Have you formed a vision for your marking and feedback practices?
- Have you attempted to get your students involved in the marking and feedback practices you have decided upon for your classroom?

Considered response:

_____

_____

_____

_____

_____

_____

_____

_____

Rate yourself

QUESTION 11: How confident do you feel in trying out new ideas in your marking and feedback practice?

1   2   3   4   5   6   7   8   9   10

QUESTION 12: Do you have an understanding of what students think of your marking?

Quick response:

_____

_____

_____

_____

Questions for consideration

- Have you sought out your students' views on your previous marking and feedback practices?
- Have you sought out your students' views on your current marking and feedback practices?
- How have students responded to new techniques you have implemented in your classroom?
- Is there anything that went particularly well or not so well when using it with students?

Considered response:

_____

_____

_____

_____

_____

_____

_____

_____

_____

Rate yourself

QUESTION 12: How confident are you that you really know what students feel and think about your marking and feedback?

| 1 | 2 | 3 | 4 | 5 | 6 | 7 | 8 | 9 | 10 |

QUESTION 13: How have you interacted with your students in terms of marking and feedback in your classes?

Quick response:

_____

_____

_____

_____

Questions for consideration

- Have you conducted any questionnaires with your students?
- Have you discussed marking and feedback with your students?
- Have you trialled out any new marking and feedback techniques with your students?
- Have you been able to plan and teach lessons where students are self- or peer-marking? If so, how did it go?

Considered response:

_____

_____

_____

_____

_____

_____

_____

_____

_____

_____

_____

_____

Rate yourself

QUESTION 13: How confident are you when it comes to involving students in the marking and feedback process?

1   2   3   4   5   6   7   8   9   10

QUESTION 14: How have you interacted with parents and carers in terms of marking and feedback in your classes?

Quick response:

_____

_____

_____

_____

Questions for consideration

- Have you conducted any questionnaires on marking and feedback with parents and carers?
- Have you discussed marking and feedback with parents and carers?
- Have you invited parents and carers in to view or discuss marking and feedback?

Considered response:

_____

_____

_____

_____

_____

_____

_____

_____

_____

_____

_____

Rate yourself

QUESTION 14: How confident are you when it comes to involving parents and carers in the marking and feedback process?

1   2   3   4   5   6   7   8   9   10

The results

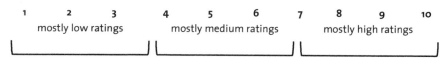

Fig. 6 How did you rate yourself?

Mostly low ratings

You still have a way to go with your marking and feedback. There is a bright new horizon that you must now work towards. You have not tried as many marking and feedback techniques as perhaps you could have done and therefore the impact on your students in the classroom and improvements in your teaching are not hugely different. You have not really read around the topic. Now is the time to step it up. You need to take the time to reflect on your marking and feedback processes in order to move yourself and your students forward. Just remember, if you always do what you've always done – you'll always get what you always got.

Mostly medium ratings

You have trialled a few new marking and feedback practices in your classroom recently and you are starting to consider their impact on your teaching and the students' learning. However, there is a huge amount that you can still do to make sure that your marking and feedback has maximum impact and moves your students forward in their learning. Now is the time to move forward and become a master in your marking and feedback practice and that comes with time, practice and focus. You have made a great start on your journey to mastery and need that practice time to hone your skills and reflect a little more.

Mostly high ratings

Don't let your advanced level in the area of marking and feedback hold you and your students back from progressing even further. If you are so effective that all of your students are getting top marks, then good for you – but is there anything that they could be doing at an even more advanced level to break new boundaries for their age group? If on the other hand, they are not all getting top marks then never stop persevering and accept nothing less. Yes they are lucky to have you, but keep them working hard. You should be training your students to be master markers now so that they can take charge of their learning and know exactly what they need to do well before they even get their feedback from you. Students can actually teach us so much about our practice if we allow ourselves to be open to their feedback on our feedback.

Now what?

It is important to decide a plan for both the short-term and long-term development of your marking and feedback practice. A good place to start your journey is by looking at and analysing the techniques and routines you have already used in your classroom or have used in the past. What worked for you and what did not go so well? Is there anything you have tried more than once and got different results with? Is there anything that was a resounding success? Looking at the why behind each conclusion you come to through your reflection is very important. Where are you now in your marking and feedback practice? What techniques do you use as standard and on a regular basis? A full and in-depth reflection on your current practice is an essential foundation for the improvements and successful changes you are going to undertake going forward so do not rush that step.

Trying out new marking and feedback techniques and routines is your second step. Your selection of techniques or routines to trial in your classroom should stem directly from your reflection on your current practice. What techniques and routines would compliment the things you do already that you are happy with and intend to continue doing? Choose a couple of new techniques or routines at a time so you can really get a feel for whether it suits you and your students and is beneficial. Make too many changes at once and you will cause confusion among your students and you will also not be able to effectively monitor whether it is working well for you. Once you have settled on a way of working that is manageable for you, stick with it and trial it out for a set time before you change anything again. Once you are happy that, for now, that is the way you want to work then it is time to make sure that your students are a part of the process and have a vested interest in making it work. The best way to do this is to involve them in it.

Teachers can be guilty of presuming that students will not ever be able to understand or mark their own and others' work effectively or at least not as well as the teacher. It is more than possible to train up your students to be excellent markers. It comes from you. You need to instil confidence in your students and their own abilities. You also need to train them well in marking and feedback in order for them to understand your marking and feedback and how they can interpret it and move forward in their learning as a result. Building up students' abilities in marking and feedback slowly, piece by piece and tying it all together as you go will really benefit the students and improve the quality of their work. The more students understand the marking criteria you use in relation to their work, the better they will be able to work towards becoming the best they can be as they will understand 'the game.' Remove the element of mystery and open up the marking and feedback processes to your students. We need to find the way to allow our students to access the success criteria that they are working within, whatever their ability. Self-belief and effective practice is a powerful thing – ensure your students have both and they are on the road to success.

Chapter 7 takeaway

Teaching tip

Keep on keeping on

Keep reflecting on your practice. You are never so good at something that you could not be better. In order for us to always be at our best we need to ensure we keep grounded, regardless of how confident we feel in a certain area. Keep looking objectively at what you are doing and how you can improve it.

Pass it on

Sharing your ideas – blogging

There are some really quite brilliant writers out there in the world of educational blogging – passionate individuals that really care about what they do and are willing to bare their teaching soul and share their experiences with the world. It is a great idea to check these out and see who you find of interest so you can then follow their writing. You can learn so much and gather ideas to use in your own practice really easily. Lots of the blog posts are very detailed and practical allowing readers to visualise the matter being discussed and take what they think is useful and apply it in their everyday practice the next day. Each chapter of this book gives recommendations of some of the great blogs that debate marking and feedback to check out, but the blogging world is changing every day so do have a look yourself. You could even become one of them!

There are some really easy blogging platforms out there that can be found with a simple search: 'how to create a blog.' The two most common platforms are www.blogger.com which is linked to Google and www.wordpress.com. Upkeep takes very little time once you have set it up. If the idea of setting up a blog yourself is a step too far, then there are platforms such as www.Staffrm.io where you can simply sign up and write individual blog posts that are shared and housed by them for you along with other educators. Why would you do this? Well, it is a great way to pass on your pearls of wisdom to the world and get some useful opinions on what you are doing in your classroom. You could journal your exploits in marking and feedback as you go, show the journey you are on and discuss the results of the choices you have made. You could set up a blog along with other staff in your school and share the writing of weekly blog posts on marking and feedback. A great way to get staff sharing good practice throughout your school as well as showing off what great things are going on in your school to parents, carers, students, teachers and even inspectors.

Share with staff
Offer to present your findings about marking and feedback since you started to be more reflective at your next whole-school meeting. It is a daunting prospect to stand up in front of your colleagues and lay bare what you are doing in your classroom, but it is so good for everyone if you are brave enough to do it. You may well inspire others to do the same. Your experiences are important and sharing them is freeing.

Share and tweet
Share your progress so far and reflections on marking and feedback in your classroom on Twitter using the hashtag #BloomsCPD.

CPD book club recommendation

Daniel T Willingham – *Why Don't Students Like School?*
(See Bibliography and further reading, page 295)

Bloggers' corner

Chris Hildrew has some fascinating posts on marking and feedback that are well worth a read. Visit his blog at https://chrishildrew.wordpress.com.

TO DO LIST:

- ☐ Reflect on how far you have come in your practice and what you still want to achieve
- ☐ Tweet the progress you have made so far and your reflections on marking and feedback in your classroom and check out what others have said by using the hashtag #BloomsCPD
- ☐ Be brave and stand up and share your progression on marking and feedback with the whole staff – you may well inspire others
- ☐ Check out Chris Hildrewut's blog posts on marking and feedback: https://chrishildrew.wordpress.com
- ☐ Read *Why Don't Students Like School?* by Daniel T. Willingham.

8

Embedding and developing the practice

Final steps

Once your research and practice have been done within your marking and feedback conduct in the classroom then it is time to think about how best to ensure long-term development and impact going forward.

Sharing with your team

Sharing your ideas and feelings about marking and feedback with your team is an important next step. However, feeling confident in your own practice is essential before you do this. Make sure you are comfortable with what you have experimented with in terms of your marking and feedback in your classroom. Reflect honestly and gather together the successes and the failures. Both sides of the story are important to share, and remember that different ideas and strategies will work for other people.

You may wish to organise a slot in your team meeting to share your endeavors. If you are not a head of department, then make sure you share what you will be talking about in detail with them prior to discussing it. They will love the fact that you are eager to improve your practice and want others to benefit too, but it is important that what you are sharing is in line with what their vision is for the entire team. If you are the team leader for the teachers that you will be sharing your newly researched ideas with, then make sure you are telling your story but also allowing everyone to see how they could use some of the ideas in their own classroom even if they do not have the same style and approach as you do. It is exciting to be on the path to improving yours and others' marking and feedback, so make sure you do it justice and inspire them too.

Action research

Action research is an enquiry undertaken by an individual that aims to improve the practice of the practitioner undertaking it. A real strength about action research is that it aims to generate practical solutions to real problems that the person taking part in the research is experiencing. It is empowering if done well and can really make a difference to the way you see yourself as a professional. It can give you a real chance to critically reflect on what you do every day in the classroom and make plans for improvement as a result of your findings. Action research produces knowledge based on investigations conducted in your classroom and allows you to analyse that knowledge and plan for improvements and development of your practice in the classroom.

When undertaking action research, you should be aiming to plan out the aim of your action research, act and observe with that focus in mind, reflect upon that observation, revise the plan and start the process again. This can be repeated as many times as you see fit in order to improve your marking and feedback, or whatever you are focusing on. You could set up some action research in to your marking and feedback practices, either as part of a supportive group within your school or just go it alone in your own classroom. This could involve analysing a set of marked books, subsequent student interaction with that marking and the impact seen. It could involve you asking others to observe a lesson in which you are dealing with marking and feedback in some way or you could record your marking and feedback lesson to watch back alone. You do not need to involve others in your action research as you can organise your research so that you trial ideas that you are doing in class and record or simply reflect upon it in a focused manner. However, the benefit of working with a group of teachers is that you can get objective feedback and also learn from their practice when you observe and feed back to them.

Forming a marking and feedback vision

Once you have really thought about your current practice in marking and feedback, it is time to form your vision for the future. Having a personal vision for your own marking and feedback is essential in these times of constant change within the world of education. Of course, your school will have its own marking and feedback policy, and it is important for the students that you adhere to it so that they are able to have consistency across their school experience and amongst the different staff they come into contact with. You can always make a marking and feedback policy work for you, but in order to do this you need to have a firm understanding of your own practice and a vision of what you want your own practices to look like in the future.

If you have this assured understanding of your marking and feedback practice then you can adapt to any students you may have in class or whole-school pressure. You need to reflect on your marking and feedback in order to form that vision.

- What do you want to achieve short term through your marking and feedback?
- What do you want to achieve long term through your marking and feedback?
- How do you want students to interact with and approach your marking and feedback?
- What impact do you want your marking and feedback to have?
- Have you tried enough in terms of marking and feedback to know what you like or dislike, and what does and does not work for you?

Embedding student-led marking and feedback

As discussed in previous chapters, developing student-led marking and feedback needs to come from a clear understanding of your own practice. Once you are certain that you have adapted or changed all that you want to about your practice, and are happy with those changes, then you can begin the process of conveying your approaches to your students and building together the confidence that they understand and are able to act effectively upon your marking and feedback. Share your routines and thoughts behind them with the students. Try all that you want to try and then get them involved too.

Make sure that you have taken these steps *before* you venture forward into the world of self- and peer-marking in your classroom.

It is a good idea to take some time to really think about what your students are already good at when it comes to marking and feedback.

- Do your students give better feedback when speaking aloud to one another or when writing?
- Are students able to be positive in their feedback rather than just pointing out one another's errors – or the other way around even?
- Are they already familiar with, understand and happy using the marking criteria you use or do they need training?

Form your plan for development around their strengths and weaknesses. Each group of students will be different, and just as when we plan lessons we need to differentiate, we need to do the same when training them in marking and feedback. Know your audience and work with their strengths. Any group of young people can become great markers and develop excellent feedback skills, but they will need you to guide them through the process.

A systematic approach

A great way to approach your student-led marking and feedback is to plan for students to complete two pieces of work close together that are assessed for the same criteria; one will be marked by you, the other by them. The first piece of work should be undertaken with the students in class, success criteria shared and adequate time given to the task. Your feedback on that piece of work should be given as soon after completion of the work as possible. The feedback should be acted upon promptly with the students looking back over the success criteria as they go. This should not be the first time you have gone through this process with the students. Ideally you will have done this multiple times so that students are comfortable with the process. It is a really good idea to talk them through the marking and feedback process as you go each and every time, repeating what you have already said to them the previous time. Students need repetition in order to learn this process and feel comfortable. If they are saying that they already know the process, as you have already told them then, get them to tell you what the different stages of the process are as you go through them; test them on their claim.

The next step is to set them a similar piece of work to the last piece you marked and gave feedback on; this is the piece of work they will peer-assess. This needs to be very soon after they have acted upon your last feedback – the next lesson if possible. In setting a similar piece of work that is assessed using the same criteria, you are allowing students to directly access the knowledge and skills that you have just imparted upon them in your previous marking and feedback. Lead them through the exact same process you have just gone through as a marker. Just as you have modelled good practice to them, in lessons, now it is their turn to emulate that good practice in their own style.

I would recommend starting with peer-assessment rather than self-assessment when you begin to involve students in the marking and feedback process. The reason being that they have to work together and discuss the process which will allow them to help one another along the way. It takes the fear factor out of the process and banishes the thought that they are doing it all wrong, when everyone else is doing it right, as there are two of them in it together sharing their experience and learning. When students are trying something new they often feel exposed, but if they have a partner in crime then it can become more of a fun challenge. You could consider grouping higher and lower ability pupils or perhaps those of similar ability together and provide differentiated supporting resources for different abilities to allow them to work together well. Pairing or grouping students to talk about and take part in marking and feedback regularly makes everyone a part of the process, even if they struggle at first.

Once they have completed peer-marking under your guidance a number of times, you can then mix up self- and peer-marking dependent on what is best suited to the task. A student being able to mark their own work effectively is a skill, as they will need to remove themselves from their own work. This process will need modelling and practice. Many students will read what they wanted to put on the page rather than what is actually written down when they look back over or mark their own work; this needs to be overtly dealt with head on before they can become masters in marking their own work. Keep allowing them time to practise their marking and feedback skills. Keep talking to them about how you mark and give feedback. Keep building their confidence in their own marking and feedback skills. They *will* become masters in their own right; some quickly and others in their own good time. It is a battle worth fighting.

Sharing good practice

Finally, consider different ways that you can work with your colleagues to better your practice in marking and feedback with the students. Just talking to other colleagues about how they approach marking and feedback is beneficial, and can help you magpie some great ideas that you perhaps would not have thought of yourself. Getting together and looking over or sharing the lesson plans where you have got students involved in marking and feedback can bring about some fascinating discussions with colleagues too. You could consider working with a colleague in planning a lesson or sequence of lessons you will both teach at the same time to your classes, and swap the student work over for another class to mark and feedback on, to get students really talking about their own and others' work. Working with others in developing your practice and getting students involved is a supportive and positive experience for all.

Chapter 8 takeaway

Teaching tip

Trust in your students' abilities

Placing your trust in students, while giving them the right support to thrive, will bring them on in leaps and bounds. Never underestimate the power of letting them see your belief in them. Allowing students to be a part of the process is so important. Once they see what goes into marking and giving feedback on a piece of work, they will value your efforts so much more.

Pass it on

Sharing your ideas – Pinterest

Pinterest is essentially a virtual pinboard. You can set up a number of pinboards for different topics and pin items to it. If you see something you like online – picture, article, blog, video – pin it to the relevant board. The item is saved as an image with a sentence below it that you can edit as you please. It is a great way to gather things that you find online about marking and feedback and keep them in some semblance of order. It is visual too, which is a refreshing change for what is essentially a filing system. You can follow other teachers who are pinning educational items and then anything they pin will appear on your homepage timeline, allowing you to decide whether you wish to pin those items too. Others can also follow you if they like what you are pinning or one of your pinboard topics.

You could set up boards for topics such as peer-marking, self-assessment, marking and feedback blogs, marking and feedback articles and education research and ideas. You could collect videos and websites that are helpful for your students in terms of bettering their marking and feedback understanding and practice and direct them towards the board as a homework or general reference point. Take a look and see what you think.

Team discussion
Try teaming up with some colleagues and planning out some lessons where you will introduce or use marking and feedback with your students. Two or three heads are better than one and can often bring up some really great ideas you would not have thought of alone.

Share and tweet
Share your experiences of developing your marking and feedback and getting the students involved on Twitter using the hashtag #BloomsCPD.

CPD book club recommendation

Doug Lemov, Erica Woolway and Katie Yezzi – *Practice Perfect*
(See Bibliography and further reading, page 295)

Bloggers' corner

David Fawcett has some super posts on marking and feedback that are well worth a read. Visit his blog at http://reflectionsofmyteaching. blogspot.co.uk.

TO DO LIST:

- ☐ Tweet your experiences of developing your marking and feedback and getting the students involved and check out what others have said using the hashtag #BloomsCPD
- ☐ Get a colleague or two together and plan a lesson in which you will involve the students in marking and feedback
- ☐ Check out David Fawcett's blog posts on marking and feedback: http://reflectionsofmyteaching.blogspot.co.uk
- ☐ Read *Practice Perfect* by Doug Lemov, Erica Woolway and Katie Yezzi

Part 2

Train others

1 Planning and preparing for your training

Before providing you with marking and feedback training plans to use in your school, we'll look at the positives of running CPD in-house. We'll have a look at the different types of CPD support that you can take part in or help organise and how you can work with other schools. This section also looks at the role of the CPD leader, something you may want to get involved with or apply for as your training experience grows, and then finishes with my top ten tips for running CPD training.

Why you should do-it-yourself CPD!

Why should you and your school run your own in-house CPD training when there are so many training resources and companies out there that you could use, implement or bring into your school with no extra hassle to you or other members of staff? Well, there are many reasons. For one, the hidden talent you have the potential to quash if you were to bring in an external trainer rather than to utilise the skills of the shy Maths NQT with a flare for marking organisation, would be a travesty – a travesty I tell you! Allowing staff to step up and lead elements of CPD across the school – from just one session on how to manage marking workload to planning a term's worth of twilight sessions – is an empowering and special opportunity. Staff who are trained by their peers, and that train their peers, will thrive and excel and the whole experience will be far more beneficial and positive than it would be with a stranger unfamiliar with the unique school context. Everyone feels appreciated and motivated because they can see that it is possible for them to be top of their game because in the CPD session last night the teacher in the next classroom was – and they are in the same school, with the same children, in the same learning context as every teacher in the training session. It also emphasises the fact that together you can form a centre of excellence without ever leaving the school grounds.

Whilst there are many well-established and very effective CPD opportunities that can be undertaken away from the school setting with positive results, there are also, of course, many below par and ineffective CPD providers and sessions out there. There are so many variables when you send a member of staff off-site for training that, if done well, on-site training can be a much better alternative. DIY CPD is the future for real and impactful staff improvement. Grow your own talent and retain your staff as your school or department goes from strength to strength.

External CPD courses

Paying for staff to go off-site and attend a day-long CPD training session has, in the past, been the main way of approaching CPD and there is a lot to be said for it (it's not *all* bad!). Positives include:

- allowing staff off-site for the day makes them feel appreciated as they are being invested in
- being away from the classroom and the school can have a rejuvenating effect on some teachers
- it allows teachers to mix with other teachers with similar interests in a topic
- sessions are (hopefully) run by an expert ensuring high-quality advice from a new perspective.

In addition, you often get a croissant on arrival and a free buffet lunch too! All of this can really make for a great day and have lasting impact for that member of staff.

The problem with sending staff off-site though, is that even if the session has a positive impact on that member of staff, it is rare for that impact to reach further than their own classroom. It does happen, but more often than not lack of time hinders the passing on of the learning to other members of staff. There is also obviously always the possibility that the training will not be of high quality or not suit the specific need of the staff member you are sending. There is no reason why we cannot emulate the experience you get from going out to high quality off-site CPD in our own school settings, and make it even better because you know your staff. It just takes a little careful planning.

Another alternative to sending individual staff out, is paying for an outside agency to come into your school and work with staff or perhaps even train the whole staff body. A fresh face with fresh ideas and no preconceptions about staff can be a great experience and really invigorate staff. However, this can be a very large expense and if the session is not quite what was wanted or is not received well, it can be a precious waste of money and school CPD time.

Top tip

There are some charities and companies such as 'Teaching Leaders' and 'Future Leaders' that run amazing programmes that I highly recommend sending staff out to take part in. They are very special and have impressive impact statistics to show for them. It would be impossible to emulate the courses completely in your own schools, but there are elements that you can absolutely bring into your own on-site DIY CPD and allow lots of your staff to benefit from. See their websites for further information: www.teachingleaders.org.uk and www.future-leaders.org.uk.

Why you should do marking and feedback DIY CPD

So why do marking and feedback CPD in-house rather than just employing an expert to tell you how it is done? For the simple reason that you know your students and you know your school setting. There is nothing more important in terms of student progression as a result of marking and feedback than knowing the students you have in front of you inside out. Of course we should look to the expert advice to guide us, but we should then absolutely use that to shape our training in our own setting, because we know best when it comes to our students and what they are capable of.

Marking and feedback, when done well, forms a very strong and important bond between students and teachers, so training staff to do it well is essential for building relationships and creating an environment where your students excel and feel supported to do so. Using internal staff to train other staff brings training to life; you can bring in real live case studies of students that they know and bring the theory into the real world. Allowing staff to see the benefit of the marking and feedback topic they are covering through the stories of the young people they actually deal with day in, day out is a real game changer.

Running your own CPD in-house, when managed and undertaken properly, is by far the most satisfying, high quality and impactful approach your school can take. There is something quite special about staff training other staff. We teachers practise our trade day in, day out and are all expert in different elements of teaching and learning. Yes, time needs to be allocated to search out and select the right staff to lead the right things. Yes, time needs to be allocated to training those staff up to be able to lead interesting and useful CPD sessions. And yes, this will be a constant, ongoing and fluid process. The person who leads CPD needs the time allocated to them to ensure that this is done well and it needs to be monitored frequently to ensure impact. But the benefits are huge!

How to choose the right teacher to lead your CPD?

You may have the task of helping to choose the right teachers to run different training sessions. The question of who to choose is a tough one, the answer to which will be vastly different from school to school. There are however, many ways that you can search out home-grown talent.

- Observation write-ups: these are a great way of seeing where different teachers' strengths lie. They are not the be-all and end-all as they are always only a mere snapshot, but they are a good place to start looking for talent in your school.
- Discussions with line managers: ask them where their team's strengths lie.
- Staff self-assessment: send out a questionnaire in which staff highlight where they personally feel their strengths lie. This can be a really useful tool to uncover things teachers feel they excel in which may not have come out in an observation for one reason or another.
- Record of external training: find out which courses different teachers have been on and encourage them to pass on what they have learnt.

Getting the right staff leading the right sessions and supporting them well is a magic formula for success in staff development and student outcomes.

Takeaway

Teaching tip
What you were searching for was right in front of you all along
Often we are searching for the expert view, perfectly written blog, most amazing course or most interesting documentary to guide our teaching practice when what we need is right under our noses! We all work so hard and have so much to learn from one another. Look around your own setting for help and advice before automatically looking towards outside agencies or educational professionals.

Pass it on

Team discussion

Host a discussion with the team you work within about where everyone sees their own and others' strengths in teaching. It may come as a surprise what staff see as their own strengths and what others see as their strengths. Keep it positive and let everyone go away feeling valued and appreciated for what they have to offer.

Share and tweet

Share your thoughts and experiences on DIY CPD on Twitter using the hashtag #BloomsCPD.

CPD book club recommendation

Ross Morrison-McGill, *100 Ideas for Secondary Teachers: Outstanding Lessons*
(see Bibliography and further reading, page 295)

Bloggers' corner

Edutopia has some high quality posts on marking and feedback that are well worth a read. Visit their blog at: www.edutopia.org.

TO DO LIST:

- ☐ Consider the strengths of the staff around you and search out help and advice from teachers you know
- ☐ Tweet your thoughts and experiences on DIY CPD and check out what others have said by using the hashtag #BloomsCPD
- ☐ Host a team discussion on strengths in teaching
- ☐ Check out the blog posts on Edutopia on marking and feedback: www.edutopia.org
- ☐ Read *100 Ideas for Secondary Teachers: Outstanding Lessons* by Ross Morrison-McGill

Supporting other teachers

Ensuring that there is adequate CPD support for everyone in a school is a very important and complex matter. There is no one-size-fits-all model that can be levered into your school CPD programme to solve all issues and allow everyone to thrive. Each school is individual and always developing and changing, so the approach needs to be selected specifically by those who know the school well. The approach towards CPD also needs to be reactive and adapt to everyone's ever-changing CPD needs and strengths.

Creating a culture of support and professional care for one another is very important in schools. Getting teachers working together and supporting one another with their CPD will lead to long-term development of those staff members and guaranteed sustained impact with the students. Below are a few ideas that get staff supporting one another and working together both generally and specifically with regards to marking and feedback. Try out using some of these methods in your training and see if you can get the ones that are most effective integrated throughout your department or school.

Coaching and mentoring

A coaching and mentoring approach to CPD gives teachers the skills to support each other effectively. Both approaches have their benefits and can be used to improve staff performance.

Coaching

Coaching can be used in conjunction with mentoring or completely separately. Coaching involves peer-to-peer discussion and careful questioning that enables the person being coached to devise their own solutions and goals for development. The coach leads the discussion but the answers and advice comes from the person being coached. The person being coached is not given any solutions, there are no suggestions for improvements and the coach provides no evaluation of their thoughts about the staff member or their practice. The coach simply facilitates the self-evaluation and self-discovery that the person being coached goes through. Coaching done well can be a powerful experience and can rapidly progress staff, especially those more cynical about the effectiveness of CPD. A coaching approach ensures that a member of staff takes ownership of their own CPD. Although it sounds simple, this does in fact take practice and training to be done well. For staff to ask the right questions to develop one another, be able to hold their views to themselves and guide the discussion without controlling it, can be a real challenge. There are many schools that are now using coaching as their main approach towards teacher improvement and who allow their staff to work towards qualifications in coaching to ensure it continues.

Mentoring

Mentoring already exists in some capacity in most schools. It involves the management of a member of staff's career progression or transition, and is often between a member of staff and someone more senior to them. The mentor has a long-term and supportive role and will often pass on their knowledge and advice to their less-experienced mentee in their new role or towards getting a new role. This can, and does, work well in most schools. The pairing of mentor and mentee is important and should be well thought out in order to achieve positive outcomes for all involved. Often a line manager will mentor their team and this is appropriate and should work smoothly if you have the right people working in the right places in your school. A staff member looking to improve in a specific area that another, more senior, member of staff is experienced in, can really benefit from mentoring and this can be an empowering experience for both mentor and mentee.

Lesson study

Lesson study is another great way of getting staff working together and supporting one another without the pressure of a more senior member of staff being present and the pressure that entails. It is essentially a cycle of goal setting, planning and designing lessons, teaching and observing lessons, and reviewing and refining goals. This can be done in groups of staff of any size, but two or three staff will work better as the cycle will be short enough that it can be done close together in a busy school term.

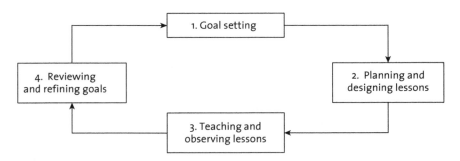

Fig. 28 Lesson study cycle

This cycle can be repeated as often as required for the desired impact.

1. Goal setting

This involves the group meeting and setting up goals that they wish to work towards in their teaching and discussing what they mean by them so everyone is clear.

2. Planning and designing lessons

This stage should be done as a group regardless of whether the staff involved are the same level or subject. Collaborative planning and discussion around choices being made will ensure that the lessons taught are understood by all and this is developmental in and of itself.

3. Teaching and observing

Staff teach the lessons that they have planned collaboratively and are observed by those that they have planned it with.

4. Reviewing and refining goals

Reflecting on how the lesson went and reviewing whether goals were achieved is essential for this cycle to be useful. This stage needs to be pressure-free and confidential to the group or staff involved – nothing to do with performance management. Done well, this can be hugely impactful and lead to staff being much more confident in their own practice.

There are many ways of approaching lesson study, e.g. it could work within a department or between people doing very different jobs from around the school; staff with similar strengths could team up or a group of teachers with different strengths could work with one another; staff at the same level in their career could work together or a group of NQTs altogether. The possibilities are endless and they all have their different benefits.

When it comes to marking and feedback, lesson study is very effective for improving whole-school practice in an individual area. For instance you could:

- focus lesson studies specifically on how oral feedback is used in the lessons that are planned, taught and observed
- conduct a lesson study plan, teach, review cycle specifically on the lessons that follow on from teachers having marked work and leading to developing the follow-up lesson in response to the marking and feedback
- use lesson study to develop peer-marking in different lessons and really enable progress in this area of practice.

Lesson study is a wonderful tool and really worth the investment in time.

Experiential CPD

Immersing staff in an experience or activity to help them understand and explore a CPD need can be a real eye-opener and can get staff thinking about one another's role on a deeper level. Organising such an experience takes time and thought, but it can have a real effect on members of staff who take part. The experience should really run itself once it has begun; the hard work for the organiser is the planning, preparation and setting up of the activities. An evaluation and discussion around the learning is always interesting with experiential CPD events, as staff discover the most surprising things when they are emerged in an experience.

The experiences can be very simple such as a member of staff teaching a lesson to the other members of staff in order to help them understand the students' perspective in the classroom. This can be used with anything you want staff to consider incorporating into their teaching practice; or indeed stop using in their teaching practice. It could also be as complex or subtle an activity as you like, such as communication games to help staff understand how important it is to communicate ideas clearly to students. Simple games such as pairing staff up and asking one to use direct instructions to help the other tie a shoelace but the person tying the shoelace only being able to follow their literal instructions (it's scary how many people simply cannot do this well) really help staff think about their in-class instructions and how they can be misunderstood by pupils if not crystal clear. Experiential CPD can be great fun and really memorable for staff.

With regards to experiential CPD for marking and feedback, you could have a group of teachers working together and have one teacher set a simple writing task which you then take in for marking. You then pass this piece of marked work back to the group and conduct a short follow-up session as if they were students in their class. Both the teacher setting the work and the teachers receiving can then feed back on how it felt and the strengths and weaknesses in the undertakings of the activity. A larger group of teachers could be set a writing task to complete and then asked to peer-mark it using guidelines that are currently used in your classrooms so that they experience the peer-marking process from the students' perspective. It is a powerful experience seeing how students view the marking and feedback process and a very worthwhile thing to do regularly to improve your practice.

Takeaway

Teaching tip
Two heads are better than one
Working with another member of staff to develop yourself can be scary, but if you allow yourself to open up and really develop you can gain so much from the experience. No one is perfect, we are all learning all of the time. Take the leap and open yourself up to collaborative development.

Pass it on

Share with staff

Seize the chance to share one strength and one weakness with another member of staff. Lay yourself bare and allow them to guide and advise you on how to improve. Choose a member of staff you would not normally ask and see if you are surprised by the different perspective you gain.

Share and tweet

Share your experiences of teachers supporting teachers on Twitter using the hashtag #BloomsCPD.

CPD book club recommendation

Jim Smith, *The Lazy Teacher's Handbook: How your students learn more when you teach less*
(see Bibliography and further reading, page 295)

Bloggers' corner

Mary Myatt has some useful posts on marking and feedback that are well worth a read. Visit her blog at: http://marymyatt.com.

TO DO LIST:

- [ ] Open yourself up to the possibilities of shared learning by trying to develop your practice along with another member of staff informally
- [ ] Tweet your experiences of teachers supporting teachers and check out what others have said by using the hashtag #BloomsCPD
- [ ] Seek out the advice and guidance from a member of staff you have not looked to before
- [ ] Check out Mary Myatt's blog posts on marking and feedback: http://marymyatt.com
- [ ] Read *The Lazy Teacher's Handbook* by Jim Smith

Working with other schools

As we have discussed, why go outside your own school setting to train up your staff on marking and feedback when you can find a plethora of resources and inspiration from within *your* own school. Your marking and feedback needs will very much stem from *your* students of course, and they should be at the centre of all that you do. Your marking and feedback style will very much come from *your* own staff and their individual personalities and styles. Sometimes however, looking outside your school is also important and teaming up with staff in another local school can really freshen up ideas and inspire people in the most unexpected ways. Having a different perspective on your approach towards marking and feedback can highlight things that may have gone unnoticed because you are all with your students and in your school every day.

CPD between schools can take many forms depending on the needs and requirements of your staff and individual school. If you are involved in organising collaboration with another school you need to think about:

- who is the best person to represent your school
- who has the right characteristics to ensure impact and a successful collaboration
- who is the best teacher to share their learning and spread the knowledge and skills they gain with other members of staff
- whether that member of staff will represent your school well and help form strong links for the future.

What you want the collaborations to look like needs to be decided in advance and reviewed upon completion. Clear processes and expectations will lead to clear and focused impactful outcomes for all involved.

What you want staff to achieve from the crossover work also needs to be carefully defined in order to meet the school's needs as well as the individual teacher's needs. It is important to remember to have clear goals and objectives when planning inter-school collaboration for staff development prior to the commencement of the training or meetings. All staff involved in the collaboration need to be a part of the planning process so that they have a vested interest in the outcome and know exactly what to expect from the experience.

Below are a few ideas to get you working with other schools and achieving together.

TeachMeets

A TeachMeet is an informal gathering of teachers and educators that follows the un-conference format; a loosely structured conference that takes on a life of its own on the day rather than in advance. Forward planning and preparation is necessary for interesting and effective snapshot presentations of great practice to take place, but the order of events and the unplanned interaction with the audience can mix things up and create some wonderfully unexpected experiences. People are invited to take up presentation slots of two minutes (micro presentations) and seven minutes (nano presentations). The emphasis within the presentations is focused on classroom practice and practical advice on teaching and learning and very often contain 'pick up and use tomorrow' tips and advice. The order of presentations is often decided on the day by picking names out of a hat. Regularly included in a TeachMeet are break-out discussion groups and games or challenges to keep the audience's energy up and get them thinking about the topic at hand. There are many variations on this format that can work very well.

Run a marking and feedback TeachMeet!

You could very easily set up a TeachMeet on marking and feedback, inviting other local schools to come along or even take part and present at the event. Focusing the entire TeachMeet on a specific topic such as marking and feedback is a great way for staff to see the depth and breadth of something they deal with every day in their classrooms. Often people do things on autopilot in their own teaching practice without delving deeply into why they do it that way. You may find that teachers volunteer a great number of sub-topics under the marking and feedback umbrella but you could also consider breaking the topic down yourself and offering a suggested list of presentation topics so that there is no repetition between presenters. Topics that could be covered under marking and feedback include:

- assessment for learning
- student-led marking and feedback
- what does not work well in marking and feedback practices
- educational research on marking and feedback
- marking and feedback as covered in the latest educational books
- top tips for high impact in marking and feedback.

The possibilities are endless. Having a hashtag for the event and encouraging tweeting as the event is underway is a great way to document the goings-on, thoughts and ideas raised during the TeachMeet. Opening up your school one evening to other local schools and hosting a TeachMeet is a great experience that can really help inspire staff to improve and foster a passion around marking and feedback.

Support and challenge buddies

Teaming up individual staff with a buddy from another school can be hugely beneficial in terms of their individual professional development and the school as a whole. Teachers at a similar level, such as two heads of department, can work together to help one another improve their own leadership and their team's performance. Having someone in a similar situation as you to discuss issues with and share ideas is a powerful tool for development. Teachers are working in isolation a lot of the time, often meaning that they can loose touch with what they are good at and what they could improve upon. Allowing staff to work with a support and challenge buddy will ensure that their practice stays fresh and that they are challenging themselves.

Before starting, it is important for both members of the partnership to state what they want to achieve from the professional link they are about to form through the support and challenge buddy scheme. It may well be that they both achieve other things along the way, but if you want them to improve the marking and feedback practice in their team or classroom for instance, then this should be clearly set out and discussed prior to the buddies working together. A few days of shadowing are a great way into this relationship. A day is allocated for each of the pair to shadow the other in their own setting, get to know one another and see how things are being done differently or similarly. Going forward, the pair can work together on progression planning for themselves or their team on agreed topics and issues. The buddies could be guided to set up inter-school or parallel projects to pursue impact with the students or their team in a particular area. They could be taught the basic principals of coaching and set up regular coaching meetings at a distance or in person to help them work through issues and gain new ideas. Having a buddy that is not in your own school can really allow a member of staff to be professionally open and honest and rapidly boost their practice.

Inter-school marking moderation can be a great way to stretch and challenge your staff and in some cases to validate their excellent marking and feedback practice too. Teaming up two heads of departments for a few hours to moderate a sample of different ability level work to ensure that they are on the ball and up to date with their marking and feedback, can be a great way to progress marking and feedback practices in areas that need it in your school.

Takeaway

Teaching tip
Broaden your horizons
When you think that you have done all that you can, then look further. Look to others in other settings to inspire and challenge you even if you do something well. We can always improve and should be looking outside our own bubble to ensure we are doing so.

Pass it on

Students on board

Working with students from another school is a wonderful experience that should be relished if it is available. Yes, kids are kids regardless of the school, but there are differences in the culture they are being taught in and those subtle differences can really challenge you if you are open to them. Share with them what your students think and take back to your school their words to share. Let the students be a part of your development.

Share and tweet

Share your experiences and ideas on inter-school collaboration on Twitter using the hashtag #BloomsCPD.

CPD book club recommendation

Shirley Clarke, *Outstanding Formative Assessment*
(See Bibliography and further reading, page 295)

Bloggers' corner

Phil Stock has some really interesting posts on marking and feedback that are well worth a read. Visit his blog at: https://joeybagstock.wordpress.com.

TO DO LIST:

- [ ] Organise a marking and feedback TeachMeet
- [ ] Consider whether you or another colleague could benefit from becoming involved in a support and challenge buddy scheme. If the answer is yes, then set it up
- [ ] Tweet your experiences and ideas on inter-school collaboration and check out what others have said by using the hashtag #BloomsCPD
- [ ] Check out Phil Stock's blog posts on marking and feedback: https://joeybagstock.wordpress.com
- [ ] Read *Outstanding Formative Assessment* by Shirley Clarke

The CPD leader

The role of CPD leader in school is a vital one; arguably the most important. Often the role is taken on by the member of the senior leadership team (SLT) in charge of teaching and learning, but not always. Ensuring that staff are appropriately and constantly challenged and supported through activities, events and training is no mean feat. It is important that whoever is given this role is adequately trained and given the time to do it well. There is no point allocating this role to an inexperienced member of staff, not training them in the skills needed and then not giving them the time to do the job. The most important tool a CPD leader needs is time. Not a few hours when there are pressure points in the year, but real time allocated every week to ensure they are able to do this role justice. A lot of heads are fearful of allocating adequate time to this role as they worry about the money they will lose by not having that member of staff in the classroom. But I say, think of the money you will save by them doing their job well!

The budget

In order to get the most from a CPD budget, the CPD leader should be overseeing and organising all CPD events going on in the school. If a member of staff is going off-site for training, then the CPD leader needs to have approved it, and ensure that it meets the staff member and school's objectives for the year. If a CPD event is going on in the school, then the CPD leader needs to have full control over how that event runs, ensure it has clear objectives linked to school improvement and that the right staff are in attendance – for every event. Whether the CPD event is a ten-minute session before school or a whole day off timetable for training, they need to have orchestrated the entire thing. By that I do not mean that they are necessarily leading every session, just that they have been instrumental in the organisation of the session. Getting the right staff working on CPD and ensuring that this is constantly reviewed, evaluated and adapted is really important. Ensuring staff are all working towards their objectives for the year and that that is in line with the whole-school agenda, every time they take part in a CPD event, is really important. Making sure that every training event is reviewed and evaluated and those findings acted upon, is also really important. This role can change everything in your school. It should underpin every other role in your school and make the staff in those roles go from strength to strength. This can be the very best job in the school if the member of staff in the role is given the space and time to do it well.

The single best thing you can do to get the most out of your budget for CPD is to ensure your CPD leader is fully supported, well trained, always backed up and given enough time to do the job well. Simple.

Outside agencies

If you choose to have an external trainer in for a day-long session, after-school event or a key note speaker at an INSET day, then make sure you are completely clear with them about what you need and want from them and get your money's worth. The worst thing you can do is pay for someone to come to your school and be left with a feeling of dissatisfaction at the end of the session. Speak with the company and be clear about what you need. There is no reason for you to have a generic CPD session from them. Every school is different so they should expect to adapt their sessions to accommodate you. If they don't, then don't ask them to run a session! Make them work for you.

There are also lots of deals to be had out there. Companies run regular promotions for schools that have not used their services before take advantage of this. If they don't overtly say they do this, then ask them. There's nothing like a good old haggle to save a few pounds! There really are some great CPD providers in existence but you need to make sure you are happy with your choice of provider and session leader. Look at reviews online, ask on Twitter for recommendations of providers, facilitators and particular sessions. Ask other schools for recommendations. There are also some free and discounted schemes for external CPD providers out there, so Google often and take advantage of offers. There is definitely a place for outside agencies in school CPD, just make sure they are the right ones and that you are still in control if you use them.

CPD tracking

Ensuring your CPD is meeting the targets for individual staff and the school as a whole is a key decider in terms of what CPD you should be implementing. If the training is right for your staff then you are saving money as you are not wasting vital CPD funds on inappropriate training or unnecessary outings. A key way to save money within your CPD budget is to ensure that you have a clear, sustainable and forward-looking tracking system. My advice to you is to throw the paper away and adopt an electronic system of tracking CPD requirements and how your staff are working towards their objectives. Whole-school priorities can be easily tracked and monitored as well as individual professional development. There are many companies out there that will do this for you and do it well, but you can do it yourself just as well if you are organised.

TeachMeets

TeachMeets are a special kind of event – that is for sure. They are free to run and can have a huge impact upon your staff. Members of staff stepping up and sharing their CPD souls to one another can be really inspirational. It does not matter if the presentations are not perfect or the points reach everyone in the room. The fact that staff are up there and sharing is not to be missed. Young or old, experienced or newbie; all are welcome to guide others at a TeachMeet and there is something quite refreshing about that. TeachMeets are usually run in the evening so there are no cover costs. There are very often prizes offered at a TeachMeet. This is a time-honoured tradition and should be up kept for the sake of fun and your staff feeling appreciated. You would be surprised how many companies are willing to donate prizes to a TeachMeet too, especially if you are tweeting during the event and they get a mention. Try contacting educational CPD providers, stationery suppliers and local businesses. A TeachMeet is a great way of bonding staff at no cost to the school whatsoever.

Days off timetable

Staff coming together for the whole day is a rarity as it has cost implications in terms of cover. If it is seen as truly beneficial to take these staff off-timetable for the day, and there are lots of occasions when this is the case, then there are things you can do to ease the money burden. Consider combining classes; divide the staff members' classes between other teachers teaching at the same time as them of the day as their classes. Staff often don't mind if it is only a few students and they know they will have the same done for them in return. Many schools have cover supervisors who cover planned class covers, and this is a great use of their time. If a cover teacher is brought in, then just make sure that you have a reliable company you use to provide the cover.

Questions for consideration

The CPD will always be a waste of precious staff time and school money if planning, preparation and thought has not gone into it. Make sure you make the right choices in CPD for your staff at the right time. Consider these questions:

- Why am I putting this CPD session on?
- What do I want to happen as a result of the CPD session taking place?
- Have I got the right person running the CPD session?
- Have I got the right people attending the CPD session?
- Have I planned how this session will be evaluated and followed up?
- How will I follow this session up once it is over?
- Is this the best use of our precious CPD funds?

The next section of the book (pp.167–294) will have a number of CPD plans for you to pick up and use with your staff and adapt where necessary to suit your setting. Whether you are thinking of running a short after-school session or a term of twilights, there is something in there for everyone.

Takeaway

Teaching tip

Do your bit to save some cash

How can you help save money from the CPD budget in your school? Think of ways you can do your bit to promote staff developing themselves without having to fork out loads of money on expensive courses. Get staff chatting with one another about their teaching and the learning in their classrooms. There is no cheaper or better CPD than a good old chinwag!

Pass it on

Colleague catch-up

Catch up with a colleague about their idea of great CPD. Think about the cost that is involved in creating what they believe has real impact. Is it doable in your setting? Is it already happening? Open the discussion around how best to spend the money you have available to train staff in your school.

Share and tweet

Share your ideas on how best to spend your CPD budget on Twitter using the hashtag #BloomsCPD.

CPD book club recommendation

Sue Cowley, *How to Survive Your First Year in Teaching*
(See Bibliography and further reading, page 295)

Bloggers' corner

Catlin Tucker has some wonderful posts on marking and feedback that are well worth a read. Visit her blog at: http://catlintucker.com.

TO DO LIST:

- [ ] Tweet your ideas on how best to spend your CPD budget by using the hashtag #BloomsCPD
- [ ] Check out Caitlin Tucker's blog posts on marking and feedback: http://catlintucker.com
- [ ] Read *How to Survive Your First Year in Teaching* by Sue Cowley

Top ten tips to get you started with successful marking and feedback DIY CPD

It's time to take everything you know about marking and feedback and pass it on to others in your school by stepping up and running some training sessions! Now is the time to put yourself forward to help train other staff within your school setting. You could think about offering to run an after-school marking and feedback CPD session, lead a department meeting focusing on training staff on their marking and feedback, or step up to speak for a few minutes about a great marking and feedback tip you have to whole-staff in a morning briefing. Whatever route you want to take in your CPD adventure, take the first step now.

Here are my top ten tips to get you started for successful CPD:

1. Get your colleagues excited about what you will be sharing with them in the session.
2. Keep focused on your objectives for the session.
3. Ensure you have 'take away' and 'use tomorrow' elements in your session.
4. Keep it focused on the students.
5. Ensure you allow time for reflection.
6. Ask your colleagues to commit to taking action once the session is over.
7. Use evidence and research in your session where you can.
8. Know your audience when you are delivering a session.
9. Don't lecture your audience; use them in your session.
10. Guide them to think deeply and get them questioning their practice.

2 Training plans

Overview

What follows is a training pack to help you improve the marking and feedback practice in your department or whole school. It is split into three sections:

1. Extended twilight

A training plan for running a one-off session on marking and feedback in your school either in an after-school twilight slot or on an inset day.

2. Twilights across a term

Six training plans intended as a series of twilight training sessions over a term.

3. Action research

A training pack for running an action research project with staff in your school.

Each training session includes three elements: a planning document, detailed session and presentation notes and a full set of editable PowerPoint slides which can be downloaded from the online resources site that accompany this book.

Planning document

This table provides an overview of everything you need to know about the individual training session. One has been provided for each session but there is also a template for the document online which you can download and fill in, adapting it to your own needs and context.

Below is an annotated example detailing what goes in each section.

Focus	Notes
Facilitators	*This section gets you thinking about whether there are any other members of staff who you might want to ask to help you with the training session.*
Topics covered	*The main topics covered in this training session.*
Preparation tasks	*The main things you need to do to prepare for the training session.*
Resources required	*All the resources you need for the training session.*
Preparation time required	*A breakdown of the estimated amount of time you'll need to prepare for each session beforehand and on the day.*

Focus	Notes
Potential problems and solutions	*Problems to keep in mind that you might face with the training session and how you should deal with them.*
Possible follow-up tasks	*Activities, events or tasks that follow on nicely from the session that could be set up or completed.*
Pass it on	*Ideas for how to share the training with other teacher in the school, in other schools or across the country/world!*

Detailed session and presentation notes and PowerPoint slides

For each training session you are provided with detailed notes on each stage of the session. It may be the case that this is the first time you have run training sessions in your school. The tips in chapter 1 of this session hopefully will have helped you start to prepare for the training. To help you further each training plan follows a similar structure which you should be able to get the hang of quite quickly. Detailed notes and extracts from the PowerPoint presentation talk you through each stage of the training. All the PowerPoints slides are available to download from www.bloomsbury.com/CPD-library-marking-feedback and are referred to in italics in each section. A selection of the PowerPoints are included in the sections themselves.

Before each session

Before getting started with each session here is some advice to think about:

Open your session with the right feel can really make a difference. Make sure that you:

- arrive at the room 15 minutes before the session starts
- set up the room exactly as you want it
- stick your seating plan on the door of the training room
- have your resources printed and ready
- put your PowerPoint on display and solve any technical glitches
- get the lighting as you want it, making sure it is suitable for viewing the PowerPoint.

Greet people warmly as they arrive. Create a welcoming environment with a positive, upbeat, yet calming presence. Consider having a thought-provoking statement, news piece or image on the projection screen as they enter. Be familiar with where people are seated so that you can direct them to the correct place if they are still unsure once they enter.

Extended twilight session

Planning document

Focus	Notes
Facilitators	• Consider whether you'd like to have any other staff members take a lead of any parts of the training session. • There may be staff members in your school who have been identified through lesson observations or performance management as particularly good at peer and self- assessment in their classroom; use them to your advantage! Get them to come along and help with your session or ask for their advise when preparing your training.
Topics covered	1. Exploration of what makes effective peer- and self-assessment. 2. Sharing of strategies to enable effective peer- and self-assessment in our classrooms. 3. Planning how to apply the ideas to your classroom setting.
Preparation tasks	• Organise the training room for how you want the participants to sit and place a list of who is to sit where at the door. • Print off the two butterfly images from the slides (attendees divided by two is the number of copies required). • Print CPD evaluation document for all staff.
Resources required	• PowerPoint presentation. • Seating plan. • Audio equipment in the presentation room. • CPD evaluation documents. • Butterfly image print-outs.
Preparation time required	**Beforehand:** • 30 minutes: Familiarisation with and adaption of PowerPoint presentation to suit your needs and teaching context. **On the day:** • 15 minutes: Printing off handouts. • 15 minutes: Setting up the room.
Potential problems and solutions	**Problem:** Some staff may feel that it is a waste of time to pass assessment over to the students as they can never do it as well as the teacher. **Solution:** The activities today should show them that this is not the case and that there is absolutely a place for peer- and self-assessment! Tell teachers that before the session or before you begin if they seem unsure.
Possible follow-up tasks	Conduct a learning walk at an agreed time to view peer- and self-assessment across the school. Feed back to all staff about the outstanding practice you saw on your travels.
Pass it on	Once staff have tried out their newly acquired peer- and self-assessment techniques in class, ask them to share what they feel worked and why in a future CPD session.

Detailed session and presentation notes

In this session you will be exploring lots of ideas around how to best approach peer- and self-assessment in your classroom.

1. Expectations and ground rules (Discussion + activity)

(Slide 2)
Take the opportunity to set the tone for the session and ensure that everyone is ready to participate actively and positively. There are a list of suggested ground rules provided but do tweak them to suit your school or personal preference. It is always a good idea to offer the group the opportunity to add any rules they feel are missing. You could ask them to write these up on sticky notes and place them on a wall for the group to view and revisit periodically through the session.

Be mindful not to skip past this stage or only skim over the ground rules, especially in the first session with a new group. Take the time to explain the reasoning behind the rules without lecturing them. The standard should be high at all times in terms of their participation as well as your delivery so share this with them. You only get the best if you give your best.

Expectations and ground rules

- Respect the views of others
- Give everyone space to make a contribution
- All questions are valid
- Actively listen
- Take part
- Confidentiality – Chatham House Rules
- Challenge the idea and not the person

Do you have any of your own you would like to add?

---

2. Aims and outcomes – adapted in line with expectations (Presentation)

(Slide 3)

Make sure you take the time to discuss the aims and outcomes in detail and answer any questions or queries that your participants may have regarding the session. This is your chance to tell the story of what is to come in the training; to get them excited, curious and interested. Put the training in context: talk about how the topic relates to your students, your school and the particular teachers in the session.

Aims and outcomes of the session

- To explore what makes effective peer- and self-assessment.
- To share strategies to enable effective peer- and self-assessment in our classrooms.
- To plan how to apply the ideas to your classroom setting.

---

3. Where are we: Our school (Presentation)

(Slide 4)

Now is your chance to ensure that everyone in the session knows exactly what has already been done, perhaps over the last two years, in your school in terms of improving peer- and self-assessment strategies. Make sure you discuss any projects that have taken place and initiatives that have been rolled out. It is important to be honest and open about what worked well and what was not so successful, so that the participants can keep this in mind when they are implementing any changes as a result of today's training. Discuss data and the impact of these initiatives and projects and whether they have been appropriate or useful.

Where are we: Our school

- What do we do well with in terms of our endeavours with peer- and self-assessment?
- What have we already done to improve our peer- and self-assessment practices?
- What do we still need to improve?
- What do we want to improve upon next?

---

4. Where are we: You (Activity)

(Slide 5)

It is important to give all participants time to self-reflect and focus on what they have done already and what they would like to focus on with regards to peer- and self-assessment. You could pause and get participants discussing on their tables

---

Where are we: You

- What do you feel confident about in terms of your endeavours with peer- and self-assessment?
- What have you already done to improve your peer- and self-assessment?
- What do you still need to improve?
- What do you want to improve upon next?

---

at this point. You could then ask for tables to feed back on various discussions they have had in their groups. Alternatively, you could ask participants to silently reflect in a journal or notebook and write about what they envision as the future for their peer- and self-assessment practice.

5. Theory (Presentation + reflection + discussion)

(Slides 6, 7 and 8)
Now that the participants have spent some time considering where the school and they are in terms of peer- and self-assessment it is time to look at some ideas and theories on the topic.

You will be taking staff through three videos clips exploring ideas around peer- and self-assessment. These are very different sides to a vast and wide-stretching debate that exists around peer- and self-assessment in the classroom. Ensure you give the participants adequate time to reflect on and discuss each of the clips.

The clips can be explored using the think, pair, share approach. This allows participants to consider the issues in the video themselves first, then build their ideas around what is being said further in a pair before eventually discussing the thoughts and ideas they had as a whole group. You could do this by selecting people at random to speak, ask for hands-up feedback or tell a representative from the pair to be ready to feed back to the group on what they talked about.

Theory

Think   —   Think about each video for two minutes.

Pair   —   Pair up with someone in your group and discuss your thoughts.

Share   —   Be ready to share your ideas.

BLOOMSBURY CPD LIBRARY

Video clips:
1 'Dr. Heidi Andrade, Ed.D. Reflects on Self- and Peer-assessment': www.youtube.com/watch?v=8OkPW_mX7Vw
2 'Self- and Peer-assessment Dylan Wiliam' www.youtube.com/watch?v=5P7VQxPqqTQ
3 'Critique and feedback – The Story of Austin's Butterfly Ron Berger' www.youtube.com/watch?v=hqh1MRWZjms

6. Show and tell (Presentation + reflection + discussion)

(Slide 9)
Take this opportunity to share some ideas with the participants about ways they can best implement peer- or self-assessment. Share with them a strategy they could use tomorrow in their classroom with their students.

Show and tell

Student marking: Reflect on your peer- and self assess-ment processes at present. What is working and what is not? Why is that? Have you shared the success criteria and allowed them to access it enough to complete this process effectively? If not how can you do this? Look at making peer- and self-marking a regular slot in your lessons to get the students used to and well-practised in the skill. I have always found that you need to train the students well in this art to get good results. Training takes time and needs clear and detailed instruction with examples given. I often live mark work on the interactive whiteboard and talk through my thinking to allow them to see how I approach the process and mark effectively before I set them off on the task.

---

7. The students (Presentation + reflection + discussion)

(Slide 10)
It is important to take some time to get the participants focusing completely on their students to remind them of the reason we work so hard to be the best we can in our classrooms: for them.

Start by asking the group how they envisage peer- and self-assessment being of benefit to the students if done well. Have an open discussion as a whole group or pair people up first; make the decision on how to structure the discussion based on how well the group has shared or reflected in the different parts of the training session so far.

This is a nice point to use some pictures of students in your school, examples of students who would benefit from the improvements that can be made by implementing any of the ideas explored today. Make it as real for your staff as possible.

The students?

This is all about making sure the experience for our students, in our classrooms, is the best experience we are able to give them. So why are we trying to improve our practice in peer- and self-assessment?

- To ensure that our students have the skills they need to work collaboratively with others.
- To ensure that our students are self-reflective young people once they leave us.

---

8. Experiential (Activity + reflection + discussion)

(Slides 11 and 12)
This is a chance to help your participants understand the importance of training their students to feed back to one another and reflect on their own work well.

Experiential

- **Person 1 – Draw a blue and yellow butterfly.**
- Person 2 – Give person 1 specific feedback on how to improve the outside shape.
- **Person 1 – Draw the butterfly once again but with no colour or detail bar the outside shape.**
- Person 2 – Give person 1 specific feedback on how to improve the internal pattern.
- **Person 1 – Add the inside pattern detail to the second draft of your butterfly.**
- Person 2 – Give person 1 feedback on how to improve the use of colour.
- **Person 1 – Add colour to the second draft of your butterfly.**

How much better is the second draft after mastery and specific feedback?

Experiential

Swap roles!
- **Person 1 – Draw a orange, black, yellow and white butterfly.**
- Person 2 – Give them specific feedback on how to improve the outside shape.
- **Person 1 - Draw the butterfly once again but with no colour or detail bar the outside shape.**
- Person 2 – Give them specific feedback on how to improve the internal pattern.
- **Person 1 – Add the inside pattern detail to the second draft of your butterfly.**
- Person 2 – Give specific feedback on how to improve the use of colour.
- **Person 1 – Add colour to the second draft of your butterfly.**

How much better is the second draft after mastery and specific feedback?

9. Practice and coaching (Activity + reflection + discussion)

(Slide 13 and 14)

With everything you have covered in today's session your teachers will absolutely want a chance to discuss everything they've learnt. Using a structured coaching method can give them a chance to explore any concerns or questions they may have around the topics covered by this point.

Practice

- Pair up in your groups and choose one person to talk for one minute about a problem they are having in relation to today's marking and feedback topic.
- The other person should listen carefully to them.
- Talk to your partner and give them as much detail as possible.

Coaching

- Once they have finished telling you about their problem, take them through the GROW process of coaching to try and see a way forward. Ask them questions to help but do not offer any answers yourself!
- Once you have finished repeat the whole process in opposite roles.

Goal	Reality	Options	Will do / Way forward
What do they want to achieve? Why do they want to achieve it?	Where are they now? What have they already tried?	What are the things that they could try? What have others tried?	What are they going to do now to move forward?

Ask participants to pair up with someone in their group and follow the process of one person talking about an issue or question they have about anything that has been explored in the session for one minute uninterrupted; then the other person leads them through a GROW coaching discussion (see slide 12). Once one person has gone through this process they should swap roles and complete the activity once again. The issue can be a simple one. Ensure you give teachers enough time to complete the process for both people in the pair.

10. Practice (Activity + reflection + discussion)

(Slide 15)
Once both people in the pair have completed the activity it is a good time to bring the groups back together for a few minutes to share the issues they discussed. Note them down and keep them for future reference and for planning of future sessions. It is right to feed back after this activity but is usually best on a voluntary basis as coaching can be a personal process to go through. Get the teachers discussing how the conversation helped them to solve their problem or if they need more help.

Practice

What was the result of the discussion in your paired coaching activity?

Consider how the conversation might help you with your issue as you go forward in your practice.

---

11. Debate (Activity + reflection + discussion)

(Slide 16)
Now that the group has reflected on their own practice, considered theories and ideas that have been researched and started to plan for improvements in their lessons, it is time to consider the different sides to the arguments surrounding peer- and self-assessment. Participants will have enough information to effectively debate the matter by this point.

Debate

'Self-assessment and peer-assessment is a waste of time and have little impact on student outcomes.'

- Side 1 – For
- Side 2 – Against

You have 15 minutes to come up with a list of ideas to present for your side and to decide who is delivering them back to the group.

Present the debate opening statement: 'Self-assessment and peer-assessment is a waste of time and has little impact on student outcomes.'

Allocate participants to one of two sides: for and against. You may choose to randomise this selection or you could ask participants to try to defend the opposite view to what they believe; it is a very valuable exercise to get them considering the opposite argument before they go back to their classrooms and implement any ideas they may now have.

Give them 15 minutes to come up with a list of ideas to present for their side and decide who is going to deliver the ideas to the group. Then conduct the debate and place yourself as the chair. It should spark some interesting discussion.

12. Review learning (Reflection + discussion)

(Slide 17)
At the end of the session, ensure that you revisit the session aims and outcomes that you presented at the start and address how each one has gone, acknowledging any that still need to be worked on and any that were achieved particularly successfully.

Once the aims and outcomes have been discussed give the participants time to reflect personally on the session and make plans for what they want to do next. This is always better done in silence for a few minutes.

Reflect and review

Aims and outcomes

- To explore what makes effective peer- and self-assessment.
- To share strategies to enable effective peer- and self-assessment in our classrooms.
- To plan how to apply the ideas to your classroom setting.

Individual reflection

- Take a minute to reflect on what you have found out in this session and how you are going to put it into action.

Follow-up

(Slide 18)

Before participants leave the session make sure to wrap the session up. Remind them of what is required of them to make this a success by highlighting what they need to commit to do following on from the session.

Follow-up

Commitment to action

- To review how I use peer- and self-assessment in my classroom.

- To take small but impactful steps to improve my use of peer- and self-assessment in my classroom.

Twilights over a term

Session 1: Theories on marking

Planning document

Focus	Notes
Facilitators	• Consider whether you'd like to have any other staff members take a lead of any parts of the training session. • There may be members of staff in your school who you know have an interest in educational studies and theory and have read around the topic. Ask these members of staff to get involved in your training session! • It is worth considering using any NQT or beginning teachers to present or discuss the learning they have done on this topic recently during their teacher training.
Topics covered	1. Exploration of the key educational theories and studies that deal with marking and feedback topics. 2. Discussion around how you can apply these ideas to your everyday classroom practice. 3. Planning for implementing some small changes to classroom practice with these findings in mind.
Preparation tasks	• Pre-reading materials shared with relevant staff at least a week prior to the session. Groups of staff selected by you receive different summaries of the thinking on marking and feedback, for example you could allocate each department a different piece of pre-reading. • Organise the training room so that attendees can sit in groups according to the pre-reading they have prepared. • Stick up a list of the topics each group was allocated at the entrance to the training room. • Print copies of the recommended web links list to hand out – to be emailed after the session. • Print CPD evaluation documents for all attendees.
Resources required	• PowerPoint presentation. • List of groups and topics allocated and seating plan. • CPD evaluation documents. • Marking and feedback bingo sheet for all staff. • List of recommended web links.
Preparation time required	**Beforehand:** • 30 minutes: Familiarisation with and adaptation of PowerPoint presentation to suit your needs and teaching context. **On the day:** • 15 minutes: Printing off handouts. • 15 minutes: Setting up the room.

Focus	Notes
Potential problems and solutions	**Problem:** Some members of staff may feel that some of the topics covered in the session aren't relevant to their subject area or the year they teach. **Solution:** Ensure that all staff know that the topic they have been given to pre-read is not the only one that will be explored in the CPD session. They will be able to choose from a range of different topics to take forward and use in the classroom.
Possible follow-up tasks	• Staff who successfully incorporate elements of new practice as a result of the discussions and learning in the session present what they have done and how it went at a morning briefing session. • Peer observations set up to watch one another trying out new techniques.
Pass it on	Start a teaching and learning blog in your school. Include anecdotes about successes as a result of the training and photos of it in action in the classroom.

Detailed session and presentation notes

In this session, you will be exploring lots of theories and ideas around marking and feedback with the teachers.

1. **Expectations and ground rules** (Discussion + activity)

(Slide 2)
Take the opportunity to set the tone for the session and ensure that everyone is ready to participate actively and positively. There is a list of suggested ground

---

Expectations and ground rules

- Respect the views of others
- Give everyone space to make a contribution
- All questions are valid
- Actively listen
- Take part
- Confidentiality – Chatham House Rules
- Challenge the idea and not the person

Do you have any of your own you would like to add?

---

rules provided but do tweak them to suit your school or personal preference. It is always a good idea to offer the group the opportunity to add any rules they feel are missing. You could ask them to write these up on sticky notes and place them on a wall for the group to view and revisit periodically through the session.

Be mindful not to skip past this stage or only skim over the ground rules, especially in the first session with a new group. Take the time to explain the reasoning behind the rules without lecturing them. The standard should be high at all times in terms of their participation as well as your delivery so share this with them. You only get the best if you give your best.

2. Aims and outcomes – adapted in line with expectations (Presentation)

(Slide 3)
Make sure you take the time to discuss the aims and outcomes in detail and answer any questions or queries that your participants may have regarding the session. This is your chance to tell the story of what is to come in the training; to get them excited, curious and interested. Put the training in context: talk about how the topic relates to your students, your school and the particular teachers in the session.

Aims and outcomes of the session

- To explore the key educational theories and studies that deal with marking and feedback.

- To discuss how to apply these ideas to your classroom practice.

- To plan how to implement some small changes to your classroom practice with these findings in mind.

Where are we: Our school (Presentation)

(Slide 4)
Now is your chance to ensure that everyone in the session knows exactly what has already been done, perhaps over the last two years, in your school in terms of studying and using educational theories dealing with marking and feedback, or in any other areas. Make sure you discuss any projects that have taken place and initiatives that have been rolled out. It is important to be honest and open about what worked well and what was not so successful so that the participants can keep this in mind when they are implementing any changes as a result of today's training. Discuss data and the impact of these initiatives and projects and whether they have been appropriate or useful.

Where are we: Our school

- What do we do well in terms of our marking and feedback?

- What have we already done to improve our marking and feedback?

- What do we still need to improve?

- What do we want to improve upon next?

---

3. Where are we: You (Activity)

(Slide 5)
It is important to give all participants time to self-reflect and focus on what they have done already and what they would like to focus on with regards to utilising educational theories and ideas to improve their practice. You could pause and get participants discussing on their tables at this point. You could then ask for tables to feed back on various discussions they have had in their groups. Alternatively, you could ask participants to silently reflect in a journal or notebook and write about what their future goals are.

Where are we: You

- What areas of your marking and feedback practice do you feel confident about?

- What have you already done to improve your marking and feedback?

- What do you still need to improve?

- What do you want to improve upon next?

---

5. **Experiential** (Activity + reflection + discussion)

(Slides 6, 7 and 8)

Everyone attending the session will have completed a pre-reading task exploring an idea or theory on marking and feedback and participants

---

Marking and feedback bingo

- You have all had pre-reading to do but you have not all had the same pre-reading to do.

- Write down the main idea that was discussed in your pre-reading in the appropriate box on your bingo card.

---

will be sitting in groups of people that have all had the same pre-reading. Now is the time to have a little fun with the aim of getting people thinking about the pre-reading that everyone else has had with a game of Bingo. All participants need to be given a bingo sheet at this point (can be printed from

Marking and feedback bingo

1. Dylan Wiliam on assessment and feedback	2. John Hattie on feedback	3. Robert Rosenthal on high expectations	4. Doug Lemov on teaching techniques
5. Doug Lemov on practice	6. Daniel T. Willingham on cognitive science	7.Ron Berger on excellence	8. Robert Bjork on desirable difficulties

Marking and feedback bingo

- You now have five minutes to find other people who were allocated one of the other seven pre-reading topics prior to the session and fill in the main idea for as many of the boxes as you can.

- There are prizes on offer for the first to get a line and the first to get a full house!

the PowerPoint); which has eight spaces for gathering ideas on marking and feedback – one for each of the eight pre-reading extracts the participants have been given. Ask the participants to fill in the space on the card that is relevant to the pre-reading they had first. A sentence in summary is enough. Then give them five minutes to get up and mingle with their colleagues talking to people who can help them fill the other seven gaps with summary sentences. Make sure you have a prize of two on offer for those who get a line and a full house. This will give them a very top line overview of the theories and ideas you will be exploring in the session today.

6. Theory (Presentation + reflection + discussion)

(Slides 9, 10 and 11)
Now that the participants have an overview of the general reading that everyone has done, you are going to show then some prompt statements taken from various educational writers and researchers around the topic of marking and feedback. Each statement can be explored using the think, pair, share approach. This allows participants to consider the issues in the video themselves first, then build their ideas around what is being said further in a pair before eventually discussing the thoughts and ideas they had as a whole group. You could do this by selecting people at random to speak, ask for hands-up feedback or tell a representative from the pair to be ready to feed back to the group on what they talked about.

Theory

Robert Bjork: Bjork believes that certain training conditions that are difficult and can appear at first to slow down or impede performance at the time in fact have greater long term benefits and better results in terms of achievement and progress.

> **Think:** Think about the statement for 30 seconds.
>
> **Pair:** Pair up with someone in your group and discuss your thoughts.
>
> **Share:** Be ready to share your ideas.

This activity is aimed at developing participant's thoughts around the discussions and research that is out there, but not to dictate how they should approach their marking and feedback. The process of academic discussion around marking and feedback should make participants think a little more deeply about the practice they undertake day in and day out often without thinking about it.

Theory statements:

Dylan Wiliam: In psychological studies, ego-involving feedback was shown to rarely be effective and at times can even have a negative effect, actually lowering achievement. He argues that it is possibly better to say nothing than to give ego-involving feedback to students. On the other hand, task-involving feedback was shown to have a significantly positive impact on student achievement.

John Hattie: He explored many issues around feedback and highlights the following as some of the most important elements for success; quality over quantity, positive student culture towards receiving feedback, disconfirmation is more powerful than confirmation in feedback, errors must be welcomed, correct peer feedback is powerful and assessments should provide teachers with feedback about their methods.

Robert Rosenthal: Teacher expectation, especially with younger students, can indeed influence student achievement. Through their study they explored the notion that reality can be influenced positively or negatively by the expectations of others. Rosenthal talks about biased expectancies affecting reality and creating self-fulfilling prophecies.

More theory statements:

Doug Lemov – Teaching Techniques: Lemov believes great teaching is an art.

Doug Lemov – Practice: Practice does not necessarily make perfect; practice makes permanent.

Daniel T Willingham: Memory is the residue to thought.

Ron Berger: We need to develop a classroom full of craftsmen. He states that this approach would mean that students work would be is strong, accurate and beautiful and they would be proud of their work regardless of their starting point or background.

Robert Bjork: Bjork believes that certain training conditions that are difficult and can appear at first to slow down or impede performance at the time in fact have greater long term benefits and better results in terms of achievement and progress.

7. Show and tell (Presentation + reflection + discussion)

(Slide 12)
Now is a great time to think about how participants could take the theory they have been discussing and turn it into real practice in their classrooms. A number of ideas about how you could transfer the research and ideas explored so far into practical everyday strategies that participants can use tomorrow in their classrooms are now shared and explained. You will need to fill any gaps in knowledge with each theory to ensure that all participants have a clear overview of the idea at this point.

You can conclude this section of the session by posing the question:

- Do you have any ideas about how best to incorporate these ideas into your marking and feedback practices?

Show and tell

Robert Bjork
Bjork believes that certain training conditions that are difficult and can appear at first to slow down or impede performance at the time in fact have greater long term benefits and better results in terms of achievement and progress.

Strategy - Repeat and weave
Interweave repetition of learning. Instead of only marking and feeding back on specific skills and knowledge in chunks, spread the learning and relearning of them over the term or year. Weave the same thread of learning along with other threads of learning so that the students are practising the skills and relearning the knowledge alongside other things. Get them to them look back over previous task and feedback that are linked so they can work on them again.

Do you have any ideas about how best to incorporate these ideas in to you marking and feedback practices?

BLOOMSBURY
CPD LIBRARY

---

8. The students (Presentation + reflection + discussion)

(Slide 13)
You need to refocus your participants on their students after all the talk about theory to remind them of the reason we work so hard: to be the best we can in our classrooms.

Begin by asking the group how they see any of the theories or ideas in practice being of benefit to the students if done well. Have an open discussion as a whole group or pair people up first; make the decision on how to structure the discussion based on how well the group has shared or reflected in the different parts of the training session so far.

This is a nice point to use some pictures of students in your school, examples of students who would benefit from the improvements that can be made by implementing any of the ideas or theories explored today. Make it as real for your staff as possible.

The students?

This is all about making sure the experience for our students, in our classrooms, is the best experience we are able to give them.
So why are we looking at theories about marking and feedback?

- To make our assessment of students even more accurate.

- To allow our students to progress even faster than they do now.

---

9. Practice and coaching (Activity + reflection + discussion)

(Slide 14 and 15)
With all the theory that has been covered in today's session your teachers will absolutely want a chance to discuss everything they've learnt. Using a structured coaching method can give them a chance to explore any concerns or questions they may have around the topics covered by this point.

Ask participants to pair up with someone in their group and follow the process of one person talking about an issue or question they have about anything that has been explored today for one minute uninterrupted; then the other person leads them through a GROW coaching discussion (see slide 13). Once one person has gone through this process they should swap roles and complete the activity once again. The issue can be a simple one. Ensure you give teachers enough time to complete the process for both people in the pair.

Practice

- Pair up on your table and choose one person to talk for one minute about an issue or thought you may have with any of the ideas that we have looked at today.

- The other person should listen carefully to them.

- Talk to your partner and give them as much detail as possible.

Coaching

- Once they have finished telling you about their problem, take them through the GROW process of coaching to try and see a way forward. Ask them questions to help but do not offer any answers yourself!
- Once you have finished repeat the whole process in opposite roles.

Goal	Reality	Options	Will do / Way forward
What do they want to achieve? Why do they want to achieve it?	Where are they now? What have they already tried?	What are the things that they could try? What have others tried?	What are they going to do now to move forward?

---

10. **Practice** (Activity + reflection + discussion)

(Slide 16)

Once both people in the pair have completed the activity it is a good time to bring the groups back together for a few minutes to share the issues they discussed. Note them down and keep them for future reference and for planning of future sessions. It is right to feed back after this activity but is usually best on a voluntary basis as coaching can be a personal process to go through. Get the teachers discussing how the conversation helped them to solve their problem or if they need more help.

Practice

- What was the result of the discussion in your paired coaching activity?

- Consider how the conversation might help you with your issue as you go forward in your practice.

---

11. **Review learning** (Reflection + discussion)

(Slide 17)

At the end of the session, ensure that you revisit the session aims and outcomes that you presented at the start and address how each one has gone, acknowledging any that still need to be worked on and any that were achieved particularly successfully.

Once the aims and outcomes have been discussed give the participants time to reflect personally on the session today and make plans for what they want to do next. This is always better done in silence for a few minutes.

Reflect and review

Aims:

- To explore the key educational theories and studies that deal with marking and feedback.
- To discuss how to apply these ideas to your classroom practice.
- To plan how to implement some small changes to your classroom practice with these findings in mind.

Individual reflection:

- Take minute to reflect on how you have found this session and what it has made you think about.

---

12. Follow-up

(Slide 18)

Before participants leave make sure to wrap up and leave them looking forward to the next session. Remind them of what is required of them to make their training a success by highlighting what they need to commit to do after today's session. Also leave them with a taste of what is to come next time you all meet together and your job here is done! The exciting process of improving their marking and feedback practice has begun.

Follow-up

Commitment to action

- Consider what you already do in your own practice from the ideas we have covered today.
- Consider what you would like to experiment with improving on as a result of the ideas we have explored today.

Next session

- We will be introducing you to the marking and feedback cycle that incorporates some of the ideas we have looked at today.
- We will be considering how we prepare for our marking.

Session 2: Preparing for marking

Planning document

Focus	Notes
Facilitators	• Consider whether you'd like to have any other staff members take a lead of any parts of the training session. • There may be staff members in your school who have been identified through lesson observations or performance management as particularly good at preparing their students for marking; use them to your advantage! Get them to come along and help with your session or ask for their advice when preparing your training.
Topics covered	1. Introduction of the marking and feedback cycle. 2. Linking the marking and feedback cycle to theories shared in the previous session. 3. How to prepare for marking in your classroom. 4. Discussion of key strategies. 5. Planning for implementation in your classrooms.
Preparation tasks	• Organise the training room for how you want the participants to sit and place a list of who is to sit where at the door. • Print key strategies help sheet (slide) for all staff. • Print CPD evaluation documents for all staff.
Resources required	• PowerPoint presentation. • Seating plan. • CPD evaluation documents. • Key strategies help sheet.
Preparation time required	**Beforehand:** • 30 minutes: Familiarisation with and adaptation of PowerPoint presentation to suit your needs and teaching context. **On the day:** • 15 minutes: Printing off handouts. • 15 minutes: Setting up the room.
Potential problems and solutions	**Problem:** Some staff may feel that following a set approach such as the marking and feedback cycle is too restrictive. **Solution:** Ensure that all staff know that they will be adapting the marking and feedback cycle to work for them. The cycle will look different in different classrooms and for different teachers. They have the freedom to make it their own.
Possible follow-up tasks	• Staff who successfully incorporate elements of new practice as a result of the discussions and learning in the session present what they have done and how it went with staff at a morning briefing session. • Peer observations set up to watch one another trying out new techniques.
Pass it on	Get your attendees tweeting during the training sessions to share the new ideas and training they are receiving.

Detailed session and presentation notes

In this session you will be exploring how to best prepare students for marking and feedback.

1. Expectations and ground rules (Discussion + activity)

(Slide 2)
Take the opportunity to set the tone for the session and ensure that everyone is ready to participate actively and positively. There are a list of suggested ground rules provided but do tweak them to suit your school or personal preference. It is always a good idea to offer the group the opportunity to add any rules they feel are missing. You could ask them to write these up on sticky notes and place them on a wall for the group to view and revisit periodically through the session.

Expectations and ground rules

- Respect the views of others
- Give everyone space to make a contribution
- All questions are valid
- Actively listen
- Take part
- Confidentiality – Chatham House Rules
- Challenge the idea and not the person

Do you have any of your own you would like to add?

---

2. Aims and outcomes – adapted in line with expectations (Presentation)

(Slide 3)
Make sure you take the time to discuss the aims and outcomes in detail and answer any questions or queries that your participants may have regarding the

session. This is your chance to tell the story of what is to come in the training; to get them excited, curious and interested in what is to come next. Put the training in context: talk about how the topic relates to your students, your school and the particular teachers in the session.

Aims and outcomes of the session

- To introduce the marking cycle.
- To link the theories discussed in the last session to the marking cycle.
- To explore how best to prepare for marking in your classroom.
- To highlight some key strategies to use.
- To plan how to apply the ideas to your classroom setting.

---

3. Where are we: Our school (Presentation)

(Slide 4)

Now is your chance to ensure that everyone in the session knows exactly what has already been done, perhaps over the last two years, in your school in terms of preparing students for marking. Make sure you discuss any projects that have taken place and initiatives that have been rolled out. It is important to be honest and open about what worked well and what was not so successful so that the participants can keep this in mind when they are implementing any changes as a result of today's training. Discuss data and the impact of these initiatives and projects and whether they have been appropriate or useful.

Where are we: Our school

- What do we do well with in terms of our marking and feedback?

- What have we already done to improve our marking and feedback?

- What do we still need to improve?

- What do we want to improve upon next?

---

4. **Where are we: You** (Activity)

(Slide 5)

It is important to give all participants time to self-reflect and focus on what they have done already and what they would like to focus on with regards to preparing

---

Where are we: You

- What areas of your marking and feedback practice do you feel confident about?

- What have you already done to improve your marking and feedback?

- What do you still need to improve?

- What do you want to improve upon next?

their students for their marking. You could pause and get participants discussing on their tables at this point. You could then ask for tables to feed back on various discussions they have had in their groups. Alternatively, you could ask participants to silently reflect in a journal or notebook and write about what their future goals are.

5. Theory (Presentation + reflection + discussion)

(Slide 6, 7 and 8)
Next you will be taking staff through the five-step marking and feedback cycle (explained in detail in Chapter 5 of the Teach Yourself section). It is up to you whether you share the whole cycle with them at this point or just lead them one step at a time through the five stages, starting with Stage 1.

Introduce the participants to Stage 1: Preparation – Preparing for marked work. Preparing students for the marking and feedback process is essential. Giving students the tools they need to succeed in a task will allow them to take control and steer their learning in the direction you need them to; rather than being dragged along by you to the finish line. In order for this to happen, careful planning needs to go into the activities and approach you take in the lead up to the students completing the assessed work.

Now that the participants have an overview of stage 1, you are going to show them some prompt statements taken from various educational writers and

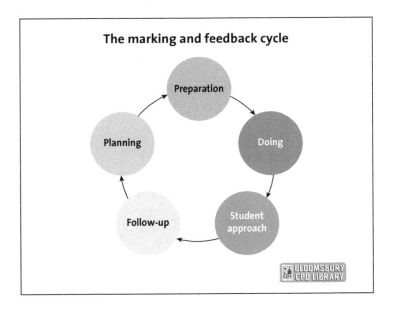

researchers around the topic of preparing for marking and feedback. Each statement can be explored using the think, pair, share approach. This allows participants to consider the issues in the video themselves first, then build their ideas around what is being said further in a pair before eventually discussing

---

Stage 1: Prepared
Preparing for marked work

Preparing students for the marking and feedback process is essential. Giving students the tools they need in order to succeed in a task will allow them to take control and steer their learning in the direction you need them to; rather than being dragged along by you to the finish line. In order for this to happen, careful planning needs to go into the activities and approach you take in the lead up to the students completing the work you will mark and provide feedback on.

Theory

Break it down – 'When presenting material to students make sure that it is clear and each element is broken down into component parts.'
–Doug Lemov

Think: Think about the statement for 30 seconds.

Pair: Pair up with someone in your group and discuss your thoughts.

Share: Be ready to share your ideas.

the thoughts and ideas they had as a whole group. You could do this by selecting people at random to speak, ask for hands-up feedback or tell a representative from the pair to be ready to feed back to the group on what they talked about.

6. Case study (Presentation + reflection + discussion)

(Slide 9)
Take this opportunity to share some ideas with the participants about ways they can best prepare their students for marking and feedback in their classrooms by sharing a case study where a teacher has used the strategies that you have just shared.

Case study

Laura is preparing her students for an assessed piece of work this lesson. She explicitly tells her class that they will be assessed on their next piece of work and that she wants them to do their very best. She makes sure the task is built up to create a little curiosity and interest in it. She builds in discussion and activity that focuses the students on the fact that mastery of the skill they need for this assessment is vital to their success. She ensures that she is clear about their prior knowledge and fills any gaps so that all students are at the same point when they start the assessment. She provides them with real life examples of what she wants them to work towards producing. She embeds in them the self-belief that if they try hard they will reap the rewards and learn faster. She explains the task clearly. She does some activities on growth mindset.

---

7. The students (Presentation + reflection + discussion)

(Slide 10)
Get the participants focusing on the students in their lessons by asking them: Why are we preparing our students for marking? Have an open discussion as a whole group or pair people up first; make the decision on how to structure the discussion based on how well the group has shared or reflected in the different parts of the training so far.

This is a nice point to use some pictures of students in your school, examples of students that perhaps would benefit from the improvements that can be made by implementing any of the strategies or ideas to prepare their students for marking and feedback explored today. Make it real for your staff at this point.

The students?

This is all about making sure the experience for our students, in our classrooms, is the best experience we are able to give them.
So why are we preparing them for marking?

- To ensure they have the life skill of self-awareness.
- To make sure that we are using our professional time as best as we can.

---

8. Experiential (Activity + reflection + discussion)

(Slide 11)
This is a chance to help your participants understand how it feels to not be prepared when encountering something new.

Experiential

To prepare or not to prepare? That is the question.

- I will now select a person at random to tell me everything about quantum physics...
- OK... I'm not that mean. If I was going to give you a tough task like that I would give you time to prepare... BUT HOW DID THAT MAKE YOU FEEL?
- Imagine how our students feel when we do not prepare them well for a task that we will mark and feed back on to them.

You need to prepare students very carefully for assessed work so that they can succeed and show their true potential. Otherwise you are not giving them feedback that will enable them to progress as their ability is higher than you realise.

---

9. Practice and coaching (Activity + reflection + discussion)

(Slide 12 and 13)
Next get attendees discussing the topics you've covered in the session. Using a structured coaching method can give them a chance to explore any concerns or questions they may have around the topics covered by this point.

Practice

- Pair up in your groups and choose one person to talk for one minute about a problem they are having in relation to today's marking and feedback topic.

- The other person should listen carefully to them.

- Talk to your partner and give them as much detail as possible.

Coaching

- Once they have finished telling you about their problem, take them through the GROW process of coaching to try and see a way forward. Ask them questions to help but do not offer any answers yourself!
- Once you have finished repeat the whole process in opposite roles.

Goal	Reality	Options	Will do / Way forward
What do they want to achieve? Why do they want to achieve it?	Where are they now? What have they already tried?	What are the things that they could try? What have others tried?	What are they going to do now to move forward?

Ask participants to pair up with someone in their group and follow the process of one person talking about an issue or question they have about anything that has been explored today for one minute uninterrupted; then the other person leads them through a GROW coaching discussion (see slide 13). Once one person has gone through this process they should swap roles and complete the activity once again. The issue can be a simple one. Ensure you give teachers enough time to complete the process for both people in the pair.

10. Practice (Activity + reflection + discussion)

(Slide 14)
Once both people in the pair have completed the activity it is a good time to bring the groups back together for a few minutes to share the issues they discussed. Note them down and keep them for future reference and for planning of future sessions. It is right to feed back after this activity but is usually best on a voluntary basis as coaching can be a personal process to go through. Get the teachers discussing how the conversation helped them to solve their problem or if they need more help.

Practice

- What was the result of the discussion in your paired coaching activity?

- Consider how the conversation might help you with your issue as you go forward in your practice.

---

11. **Review learning** (Reflection + discussion)

(Slide 15)

At the end of the session, ensure that you revisit the session aims and outcomes that you presented at the start and address how each one has gone, acknowledging any that still need to be worked on and any that were achieved particularly successfully.

Once the aims and outcomes have been discussed give the participants time to reflect personally on the session today and make plans for what they want to do next. This is always better done in silence for a few minutes.

Reflect and review

Aims and outcomes

- To introduce the marking cycle.
- To link the theories discussed in the last session to the marking cycle.
- To explore how best to prepare for marking in your classroom.
- To highlight some key strategies to use.
- To plan how to apply the ideas to your classroom setting.

Individual reflection

- Take a minute to reflect on how you have found this session and what it has made you think about.

---

12. **Follow-up**

(Slide 16)

Before participants leave make sure to wrap up and leave them looking forward to the next session. Remind them of what is required of them to make their training a success by highlighting what they need to commit to do after today's session. Also leave them with a taste of what is to come next time you all meet together and your job here is done!

Follow-up

Commitment to action

- Prepare your students well for work you are going to assess them on in your lessons.

Next session

- To look at the most effective ways to cope with conducting marking and feedback.

Twilight Session 3: Doing marking

Focus	Notes
Facilitators	• Consider whether you'd like to have any other staff members take a lead of any parts of the training session. • There may be learning support staff that have a real interest in taking on more marking responsibility. Often teaching assistants/learning support assistants/classroom assistants are a highly underused invaluable help in this area; ask them to help you with the training.
Topics covered	1. Introduction of 'Stage 2: Doing' part of the marking and feedback cycle as a possible way of approaching marking and feedback. 2. How to prepare for marking in your classroom. 3. Discussion of key strategies. 4. Planning for implementation in the classroom.
Preparation tasks	• Organise the training room for how you want the participants to sit and place a list of who is to sit where at the door. • Print key strategies help sheet (slide) for all staff. • Print CPD evaluation documents for all staff.
Resources required	• PowerPoint presentation. • Seating plan. • CPD evaluation documents. • Key strategies help sheet.
Preparation time required	**Beforehand:** • 30 minutes: Familiarisation with and adaptation of PowerPoint presentation to suit your needs and teaching context. **On the day:** • 15 minutes: Printing off handouts. • 15 minutes: Setting up the room.
Potential problems and solutions	**Problem:** Some participants may already have a marking style that they use and like and don't want to change. **Solution:** Reassure participants that they can tweak their style to make it even better through using the advice covered in the session. They do not need to start again form scratch. This approach takes theory into consideration so is worth a try.
Possible follow-up tasks	Staff can moderate the marking going on in their department once they try out some of the techniques suggested to see how others approached it.
Pass it on	Hold a TeachMeet in your school! You could invite teachers from other local schools along too. The TeachMeet could showcase some of the great things going on around the school in terms of marking and feedback.

Detailed session and presentation notes

In this session you will be looking at how to undertake marking and feedback in your classroom: the 'doing'.

1. Expectations and ground rules (Discussion + activity)

(Slide 2)
Take the opportunity to set the tone for the session and ensure that everyone is ready to participate actively and positively. There are a list of suggested ground rules provided but do tweak them to suit your school or personal preference. It is always a good idea to offer the group the opportunity to add any rules they feel are missing. You could ask them to write these up on sticky notes and place them on a wall for the group to view and revisit periodically through the session.

Expectations and ground rules

- Respect the views of others
- Give everyone space to make a contribution
- All questions are valid
- Actively listen
- Take part
- Confidentiality – Chatham House Rules
- Challenge the idea and not the person

Do you have any of your own you would like to add?

 BLOOMSBURY CPD LIBRARY

---

2. Aims and outcomes – adapted in line with expectations (Presentation)

(Slide 3)
Make sure you take the time to discuss the aims and outcomes of the session in detail and answer any questions or queries that attendees may have. This is your chance to tell the story of what is to come in the training; to get them excited, curious and interested. Put the training in context: talk about how the topic relates to your students, your school and the particular teachers in the session.

Aims and outcomes of the session

- To introduce the 'doing' stage of the marking and feedback cycle.

- To highlight some key strategies to use.

- To plan how to apply the strategies to your classroom setting.

---

3. Where are we: Our school (Presentation)

(Slide 4)
Now is your chance to ensure that everyone in the session knows exactly what has already been done, perhaps over the last two years, in your school in terms of improving marking practice. Make sure you discuss any projects that have taken place and initiatives that have been rolled out. It is important to be honest and open about what worked well and what was not so successful so that the participants can keep this in mind when they are implementing any changes as a result of today's training. Discuss data and the impact of these initiatives and projects and whether they have been appropriate or useful.

Where are we: Our school

- What do we do well with in terms of our marking and feedback?

- What have we already done to improve our marking and feedback ?

- What do we still want to improve?

- What do we want to improve upon next?

---

4. Where are we: You (Activity)

(Slide 5)

It is important to give all participants time to self-reflect and focus on what they have done already and what they would like to focus on with regards to improving

---

Where are we: You

- What areas of your marking and feedback practice do you feel confident about?

- What have you already done to improve your marking and feedback ?

- What do you still need to improve?

- What do you want to improve upon next?

---

their marking practice. You could pause and get participants discussing on their tables at this point. You could then ask for tables to feed back on various discussions they have had in their groups. Alternatively, you could ask participants to silently reflect in a journal or notebook and write about what their future goals are.

5. Theory (Presentation + reflection + discussion)

(Slides 6, 7, 8 and 9)
In this session you will be taking staff through the second step of the five-step marking and feedback cycle.

Now that the participants have an overview of stage 2, you are going to show them some prompt statements taken from various educational writers and researchers around the topic of marking and feedback. Each statement can be explored using the think, pair, share approach. This allows participants to really consider the statement themselves first, then build their ideas around what is being said further in a pair before eventually bringing the whole group back together again to gather thoughts and ideas. You could do this by selecting people at random to speak, ask for hands-up feedback or tell a representative from the pair to be ready to feed back to the group on what they talked about.

Stage 2:
Doing marking

Once students have completed the work that you have prepared them so well for, the task of actually getting down to it and doing the marking and feedback is all yours. Hopefully the students' work will be of a high quality because they were well prepared for it in your lessons leading up to the assessed work. Now is the time to do it justice and provide high quality, low effort, high impact marking and feedback that will enable your students to progress and improve. How you approach the marking will very much depend on the type of task the students have completed and what you are assessing.

Theory

'...the change in the teachers' expectations regarding the intellectual performance of these allegedly 'special' children had led to an actual change in the intellectual performance of these randomly selected children.' - Robert Rosenthal

Think: Think about statement for 30 seconds.

Pair: Pair up with someone in your group and discuss your thoughts.

Share: Be ready to share your ideas.

Theory

Ego-involving feedback can include students receiving grades where they can compare themselves with others in the class or organizing praise. Task-involving feedback focuses more on steps for improvement in that particular task and how they might go about this. In psychological studies, ego-involving feedback was shown to rarely be effective and at times can even have a negative effect, actually lowering achievement. He argues that it is possibly better to say nothing than to give ego-involving feedback to students – Dylan William

Think: Think about statement for 30 seconds.

Pair: Pair up with someone in your group and discuss your thoughts.

Share: Be ready to share your ideas.

6. Show and tell (Presentation + reflection + discussion)

(Slide 10)
Take this opportunity to share some ideas with the participants about ways they can best undertake marking and feedback for maximum impact by sharing a possible strategy they could try using.

Show and tell

No grades

Look at your marking and assessing and decide whether you give more task-involving or ego-involving feedback and assess which has more impact in the books. Do you use grades too often? Consider not providing students with grades or withholding them until certain points during the year. If you are required to grade, is there a way you could withhold the grades and ask students to act upon your feedback before you let them know their grade?

---

7. The students (Presentation + reflection + discussion)

(Slide 11)
Get participants focusing on the students in their lessons by asking them: Why are we trying to improve the way we do our marking? Then have a group discussion about how they see the ideas you've discussed being of benefit to the students if done well. Have an open discussion as a whole group or pair people up first.

This is a nice point to use some pictures of students in your school, examples of students that perhaps would benefit from the improvements that can be made by implementing any of the strategies or ideas to prepare their students for marking and feedback explored today. Make it real for your staff at this point.

The students?

This is all about making sure the experience for our students, in our classrooms, is the best experience we are able to give them. So why are we trying to improve the way we do our marking?

To ensure that we give our students feedback that will enable them to progress as much as possible.

---

8. Experiential (Activity + reflection + discussion)

(Slide 12)

This is a chance to help attendees understand the importance of giving high quality feedback to ensure high quality progress for your students.

Experiential

Image game

- One of you has an image. Your job is to give as much high quality feedback as you can to make the other person's representation of it as high quality as possible.
- Firstly, the person who has not seen the image must draw the following thing – a garden.
- Secondly, you should give them as much detailed feedback as possible to make the image look like yours and they need to draw it again.
- Finally, you must given them feedback again without showing them the image.

  You will need to be as specific as you can to enable students to progress as a result of your feedback.

Get them playing the image game.

9. Practice and coaching
(Activity + reflection + discussion)

(Slide 13 and 14)
With all the theory that has been covered in today's session your teachers will absolutely want a chance to discuss everything they've learnt. Using a structured coaching method can give them a chance to explore any concerns or questions they may have around the topics covered by this point.

Ask participants to pair up with someone in their group and follow the process of one person talking about an issue or question they have about anything that has been explored today for one minute uninterrupted; then the other person leads them through a GROW coaching discussion (see slide 13). Once one person has gone through this process they should swap roles and complete the activity once again. The issue can be a simple one. Ensure you give teachers enough time to complete the process for both people in the pair.

Practice

- Pair up in your groups and choose one person to talk for one minute about a problem they are having in relation to today's marking and feedback topic.

- The other person should listen carefully to them.

- Talk to your partner and give them as much detail as possible.

Coaching

- Once they have finished telling you about their problem, take them through the GROW process of coaching to try and see a way forward. Ask them questions to help but do not offer any answers yourself!
- Once you have finished repeat the whole process in opposite roles.

Goal	Reality	Options	Will do / Way forward
What do they want to achieve? Why do they want to achieve it?	Where are they now? What have they already tried?	What are the things that they could try? What have others tried?	What are they going to do now to move forward?

10. Practice (Activity + reflection + discussion)

(Slide 15)

Once both people in the pair have completed the activity it is a good time to bring the groups back together for a few minutes to share the issues they discussed.

Practice

- What was the result of the discussion in your paired coaching activity?

- Consider how the conversation might help you with your issue as you go forward in your practice.

Note them down and keep them for future reference and for planning of future sessions. It is right to feed back after this activity but is usually best on a voluntary basis as coaching can be a personal process to go through. Get the teachers discussing how the conversation helped them to solve their problem or if they need more help.

11. Review learning (Reflection + discussion)

(Slide 16)
At the end of the session, ensure that you revisit the session aims and outcomes that you presented at the start and address how each one has gone, acknowledging any that still need to be worked on and any that were achieved particularly successfully.

Once the aims and outcomes have been discussed give the participants time to reflect personally on the session today and make plans for what they want to do next. This is always better done in silence for a few minutes.

Reflect and review

Aims and outcomes
- To introduce the 'doing' stage of the marking and feedback cycle.
- To highlight some key strategies to use.
- To plan how to apply the strategies to your classroom setting.

Individual reflection
- Take a minute to reflect on how you have found this session and what it has made you think about.

---

12. Follow-up

(Slide 17)

Before participants leave make sure to wrap up and leave them looking forward to the next session. Remind them of what is required of them to make their training a success by highlighting what they need to commit to do after today's session. Also leave them with a taste of what is to come next time you all meet together and your job here is done! The exciting process of improving their marking and feedback practice has begun.

Follow-up

Commitment to action

- Consider your marking practice and set yourself some targets for improving and refining your practice.

Next session

- Explore the manner in which students approach the marking and feedback they receive in your classrooms.

Twilight Session 4: Student approach to marking

Planning document

Focus	Notes
Facilitators	• Consider whether you'd like to have any other staff members take a lead of any parts of the training session. • For this session it would be nice to bring in a couple of student representatives to talk to the teachers about their experience of making and feedback. After all, this session is all about them.
Topics covered	1. Exploration of how students approach the marking and feedback they receive. 2. Discussion of key strategies. 3. Planning for implementation in the classroom.
Preparation tasks	• Organise the training room for how you want the participants to sit and place a list of who is to sit where at the door. • Print key strategies help sheet (slide) for all staff. • Print CPD evaluation documents for all staff.
Resources required	• PowerPoint presentation. • Seating plan. • CPD evaluation documents. • Key strategies help sheet.
Preparation time required	**Beforehand:** • 30 minutes: Familiarisation with and adaptation of PowerPoint presentation to suit your needs and teaching context. • 15 minutes: Prepare the student speakers (if you choose to have them in the session). **On the day:** • 15 minutes: Printing off handouts. • 15 minutes: Setting up the room. • 10 minutes: Making sure all your student speakers have arrived and know what they're doing.
Potential problems and solutions	**Problems:** Some participants may be doubtful about the ability of some of their students to respond appropriately to the feedback they are given. **Solution:** Staff need to be reassured that they have the power to create the climate for excellent and impactful marking and feedback in their classrooms – for every student. They should be reminded that repetition is the key here. Students need time and practice to get their approach to marking and feedback right and it is up to them to structure that process for them by showing them the way to do it.
Possible follow-up tasks	Student surveys could be conducted to investigate students' thoughts and feelings about marking and feedback. This could be done either by individual teachers or on a whole-school level and the results shared with staff.
Pass it on	How about setting up a hashtag on Twitter for your marking and feedback CPD sessions? Staff can then easily look back and find relevant tweets from the sessions as they will all be bookmarked with the same hashtag. (You could use our hashtag: and see what other schools have been up to as well!)

Detailed session and presentation notes

In this session you will be exploring how best to improve student approaches to marking and feedback with the teachers in this session.

1. Expectations and ground rules (Discussion + activity)

(Slide 2)
Take the opportunity to set the tone for the session and ensure that everyone is ready to participate actively and positively. There are a list of suggested ground rules provided but do tweak them to suit your school or personal preference. It is always a good idea to offer the group the opportunity to add any rules they feel are missing. You could ask them to write these up on sticky notes and place them on a wall for the group to view and revisit periodically through the session.

Expectations and ground rules

- Respect the views of others
- Give everyone space to make a contribution
- All questions are valid
- Actively listen
- Take part
- Confidentiality – Chatham House Rules
- Challenge the idea and not the person

Do you have any of your own you would like to add?

---

2. Aims and outcomes – adapted in line with expectations (Presentation)

(Slide 3)
Make sure you take the time to discuss the aims and outcomes in detail and answer any questions or queries that your participants may have regarding the session. This is your chance to tell the story of what is to come in the training; to get them excited, curious and interested in what is to come next. Put the training in context: talk about how the topic relates to your students, your school and the particular teachers in the session.

Aims and outcomes of the session

- To explore how students approach the marking and feedback they receive in your classrooms.

- To highlight some key strategies to use.

- To plan how to apply the ideas to your classroom setting.

 BLOOMSBURY CPD LIBRARY

---

3. Where are we: Our school (Presentation)

(Slide 4)
Now is your chance to ensure that everyone in the session knows exactly what has already been done, perhaps over the last two years, in your school in terms of improving students' approach to marking. Make sure you discuss any projects that have taken place and initiatives that have been rolled out. It is important to be honest and open about what worked well and what was not so successful, so that the participants can keep this in mind when they are implementing any changes as a result of today's training. Discuss data and the impact of these initiatives and projects and whether they have been appropriate or useful.

Where are we: Our school

- What do we do well with in terms of our marking and feedback?

- What have we already done to improve our marking and feedback?

- What do we still need to improve?

- What do we want to improve upon next?

4. Where are we: You (Activity)

(Slide 5)
It is important to give all participants time to self-reflect and focus on what they have done already and what they would like to focus on with regards

Where are we: You

- What areas of your marking and feedback do you feel confident about?

- What have you already done to improve your marking and feedback?

- What do you still need to improve?

- What do you want to improve upon next?

to improving their students' approach to marking. You could pause and get participants discussing on their tables at this point. You could then ask for tables to feed back on various discussions they have had around the tables. Alternatively, you could ask participants to silently reflect in a journal or notebook and write about what their future goals are.

5. Theory (Presentation + reflection + discussion)

(Slide 6, 7, 8 and 9)
You will be taking staff through the third step of the five-step marking and feedback cycle.

Now that the participants have an overview of Stage 3 you are going to show then some prompt statements taken from various educational writers and researchers around the topic of student approaches to marking and feedback. Each statement can be explored using the think, pair, share approach. This allows participants to really consider the statement themselves first, then build their ideas around what is being said further in a pair before eventually bringing the whole group back together again to gather thoughts and ideas. You could do this by selecting people at random to speak, ask for hands-up feedback or tell a representative from the pair to be ready to feed back to the group on what they talked about.

Stage 3: Student approach
Student approach to marking

The manner in which students approach the marking and feedback in your lessons can be very telling. **It takes time, effort and lots of practice to implement a culture of excellence and pride in the work that students produce and an open mind to advice and guidance given in response to it.** You create the culture in your classroom when it comes to marking and feedback and how it is received. Even the most challenging class can be trained to appreciate the feedback they get and really begin to progress as a result: it just takes perseverance. The mistake a lot of teachers make is lack of repetition of the teaching of the skills necessary to approach and respond to feedback given. This needs to be repeated and demonstrated multiple times even with classes who initially respond well to the process in order for it to be continually effective. Don't become complacent with an apparent 'good class' that appear to pick it up quickly; keep pushing them.

Theory

Hattie talks of the importance of student expectation or student self reported grades. He notes, in Visible Learning, the importance of students being able to become aware of their own expectations on themselves and then encouraged to exceed these to ensure motivation and subsequent progression.
- John Hattie

Think: Think about the statement for 30 seconds.

Pair: Pair up with someone in your group and discuss your thoughts.

Share: Be ready to share your ideas.

Theory

Dweck says that 'For students of a growth mindset, it doesn't make sense to stop trying. For them, adolescence is a time of opportunity: a time to learn new subjects, a time to find out what they want to become in the future.' She advocates the importance and impact cultivating growth mindsets can have.
– Carol Dweck

Think: Think about the statement for 30 seconds.

Pair: Pair up with someone in your group and discuss your thoughts.

Share: Be ready to share your ideas.

6. **Show and tell** (Presentation + reflection + discussion)

(Slide 10)
Take this opportunity to share some ideas with the participants about ways they can best enable students to best approach your marking and feedback by sharing with them some ideas to consider on the topic...

Show and tell

Student approach

How do your students presently respond to marking and feedback when they receive it? You could consider having some sessions and discussions around the point of marking and how best to approach it. Train them up to take marking and feedback as they should - a developmental process and not merely criticism. Do students have high expectations of themselves and know how to achieve and exceed these expectations? If not, make sure you provide them with the tools to do this in your classroom.

7. **The students** (Presentation + reflection + discussion)

(Slide 11)
Get participants focusing on the students in their lessons by asking them: Why are we trying to improve the way students approach our marking and feedback? Then have a group discussion about how they see the ideas you've discussed being of benefit to the students if done well. Have an open discussion as a whole group or pair people up first.

This is a nice point to use some pictures of students in your school, examples of students that perhaps would benefit from the improvements that can be made by implementing any of the strategies or ideas to prepare their students for marking and feedback explored today. Make it real for your staff at this point.

The students?

This is all about making sure the experience for our students, in our classrooms, is the best experience we are able to give them. So why are we trying to improve our students' approach to marking and feedback?

To ensure that our students leave us ready to take advice and make improvements.

---

8. Experiential (Activity + reflection + discussion)

(Slide 12)

This is a chance to make your participants understand the importance of forming a positive student approach to marking in the classrooms.

Experiential

The Mindset Switch

- As a group of four go around the circle and tell the group about some thing you cannot do.
- As a group again go around the circle and tell the group about this thing that you cannot do but add yet at the end of the sentence and say it three times slowly with increasing enthusiasm.

You will need to motivate students to believe they can do what they think they cannot do. Language can be very powerful. Think about how you want to use it I your classroom.

---

9. Practice and coaching (Activity + reflection + discussion)

(Slide 13 and 14)

With everything that's been covered in today's session your teachers will absolutely want a chance to discuss everything they've learnt. Using a structured coaching method can give them a chance to explore any concerns or questions they may have around the topics covered by this point.

Practice

- Pair up in your groups and choose one person to talk for one minute about a problem they are having in relation to today 's marking and feedback topic.

- The other person should listen carefully to them.

- Talk to your partner and give them as much detail as possible.

Coaching

- Once they have finished telling you about their problem, take them through the GROW process of coaching to try and see a way forward. Ask them questions to help but do not offer any answers yourself!

- Once you have finished repeat the whole process in opposite roles.

Goal	Reality	Options	Will do / Way forward
What do they want to achieve? Why do they want to achieve it?	Where are they now? What have they already tried?	What are the things that they could try? What have others tried?	What are they going to do now to move forward?

Ask participants to pair up with someone in their group and follow the process of one person talking about an issue or question they have about anything that has been explored today, for one minute uninterrupted; then the other person leads them through a GROW coaching discussion (see slide 13). Once one person has gone through this process they should swap roles and complete the activity once again. The issue can be a simple one. Ensure you have give teachers enough time to complete the process for both people in the pair.

10. Practice (Activity + reflection + discussion)

(Slide 15)
Once both people in the pair have completed the activity it is a good time to bring the groups back together for a few minutes to share the issues they discussed. Note them down and keep them for future reference and for planning of future sessions. It is right to feed back after this activity but is usually best on a voluntary basis as coaching can be a personal process to go through. Get the teachers discussing how the conversation helped them to solve their problem or if they need more help.

Practice

- What was the result of the discussion in your paired coaching activity?

- Consider how the conversation might help you with your issue as you go forward in your practice.

---

11. Review learning (Reflection + discussion)

(Slide 16)

At the end of the session, ensure that you revisit the session aims and outcomes that you presented at the start and address how each one has gone, acknowledging any that still need to be worked on and any that were achieved particularly successfully.

Once the aims and outcomes have been discussed give the participants time to reflect personally on the session today and make plans for what they want to do next. This is always better done in silence for a few minutes.

Reflect and review

Aims

- To explore how students approach the marking and feedback they receive in your classrooms.
- To highlight some key strategies to use.
- To plan how to apply the ideas to your classroom setting.

Individual reflection

- Take a minute to reflect on how you have found this session and what it has made you think about.

---

12. Follow-up

(Slide 17)

Before participants leave make sure to wrap up and leave them looking forward to the next session. Remind them of what is required of them to make their training a success by highlighting what they need to commit to do after today's session. Also leave them with a taste of what is to come next time you all meet together and your job here is done!

Follow-up

Commitment to action

- To review the tasks you set following marking and ensure that they are designed to further embed learning and encourage mastery.

Next session

- Explore the manner in which students approach the marking and feedback they receive in your classrooms.

Twilight Session 5: Follow-up to marking

Planning document

Focus	Notes
Facilitators	• Consider whether you'd like to have any other staff members take a lead of any parts of the training session. • Consider inviting some of your school's department heads to come to the training session and talk briefly about the follow-up to marking tasks they organise in their department.
Topics covered	1. Exploration of how best to design effective and impactful follow-up tasks once marking and feedback has been given to students. 2. Key strategies discussed. 3. Planning for implementation in the classroom.
Preparation tasks	• Organise the training room for how you want the participants to sit and place a list of who is to sit where at the door. • Print key strategies help sheet (slide) for all staff. • Print CPD evaluation document for all staff.
Resources required	• PowerPoint presentation. • Seating plan. • CPD evaluation documents. • Key strategies help sheet.
Preparation time required	**Beforehand:** • 30 minutes: Familiarisation with and adaption of PowerPoint to suit the needs of your particular context. **On the day:** • 15 minutes: Printing off handouts. • 15 minutes: Setting up the room.
Potential problems and solutions	**Problem:** Some participants may be concerned that it will be boring for students to just repeat the work every time they are given feedback on something. **Solution:** Staff need to be reassured that the activities and suggestions they will explore today will allow them to vary the student follow-up task without doing lots of different activities just for the sake of it.
Possible follow-up tasks	Staff can feed back on what they have done as marking and feedback follow-up tasks in their classrooms and a whole-school list of possible follow-up tasks can be collated and shared for all to benefit.
Pass it on	Write a letter to parents and carers informing them about the whole-school focus on improving marking and feedback to ensure that their children get the very best teaching that the school can offer. Parents and carers love to be kept in the loop when the school is really trying to do something to better their children's education.

In this session you will be exploring lots of ideas around how best to follow-up marking and feedback with the teachers.

1. **Expectations and ground rules** (Discussion + activity)

(Slide 2)

Take the opportunity to set the tone for the session and ensure that everyone is ready to participate actively and positively. There are a list of suggested ground rules provided but do tweak them to suit your school or personal preference. It is always a good idea to offer the group the opportunity to add any rules they feel are missing. You could ask them to write these up on sticky notes and place them on a wall for the group to view and revisit periodically through the session.

Expectations and ground rules

- Respect the views of others
- Give everyone space to make a contribution
- All questions are valid
- Actively listen
- Take part
- Confidentiality – Chatham House Rules
- Challenge the idea and not the person

Do you have any of your own you would like to add?

---

2. **Aims and outcomes – adapted in line with expectations** (Presentation)

(Slide 3)

Make sure you take the time to discuss the aims and outcomes in detail and answer any questions or queries that your participants may have regarding the session. This is your chance to tell the story of what is to come in the training: to get them excited, curious and interested in what is to come next. Put the training in context: talk about how the topic relates to your students, your school and the particular teachers in the session.

Aims and outcomes of the session

- To explore how students approach the marking and feedback they receive in your classrooms.

- To highlight some key strategies to use.

- To plan how to apply the ideas to your classroom setting.

3. Where are we: Our school (Presentation)

(Slide 4)

Now is your chance to ensure that everyone in the session knows exactly what has already been done, perhaps over the last two years, in your school in terms of

Where are we: Our school

- What do we do well with in terms of our marking and feedback?

- What have we already done to improve our marking and feedback?

- What do we still need to improve?

- What do we want to improve upon next?

improving follow-up to marking tasks. Make sure you discuss any projects that have taken place and initiatives that have been rolled out. It is important to be honest and open about what worked well, and what was not so successful, so that the participants can keep this in mind when they are implementing any changes as a result of today's training. Discuss data and the impact of these initiatives and projects and whether they have been appropriate or useful.

4. **Where are we: You** (Activity)

(Slide 5)
It is important to give all participants time to self-reflect and focus on what they have done already and what they would like to focus on with regards to improving their follow-up to marking tasks. You could pause and get participants discussing on their tables at this point. You could then ask for tables to feed back on various discussions they have had in their groups. Alternatively, you could ask participants to silently reflect in a journal or notebook and write about what their future goals are.

Where are we: You

- What do you feel confidence about in terms of your marking and feedback?

- What have you already done to improve your marking and feedback?

- What do you still need to improve?

- What do you want to improve upon next?

---

5. **Theory** (Presentation + reflection + discussion)

(Slide 6, 7, 8 and 9)

You will be taking staff through the second step of the five step cycle outlined in the diagram below (explained in detail in the first half of this book) so it is your choice as to whether you share the cycle with them at this point or just lead them one step at a time through the cycle in the training sessions.

Stage 4
Follow-up to marking

Once students have been given time and space to read, reflect and take in your marking and feedback it is important to give them time to take steps in line with your advice and guidance. It is advisable to do this as soon as possible, preferably in the same lesson that they receive the marking and feedback. Providing them with as activity that makes them think about what you have fed back to them and try to implement any advice is the best way to get hem to progress in their learning and ensure that they are able to take on board all the comments they receive. Getting a routine in place whereby student know what to expect when they get feedback on their work and can practice getting better at responding to and acting upon it will mean you don't have to do all the work; they will be able to lead themselves through the process after a while.

Theory

Do It Again - Doing it again and doing it right, better or perfect.
Precise Praise - ensure that praise is precise and used when it is deserved.
-Doug Lemov

> **Think:** Think about the statement for 30 seconds.
>
> **Pair:** Pair up with someone in your group and discuss your thoughts.
>
> **Share:** Be ready to share your ideas.

Theory

Berger sets out five pedagogical principles that be believes help create a culture of excellence; assigning work that matters; study examples of excellence; build a culture of kind, specific and helpful critique; require multiple revisions and redrafts; provide opportunities for public presentation.
– Ron Berger

Think: Think about the statement for 30 seconds.

Pair: Pair up with someone in your group and discuss your thoughts.

Share: Be ready to share your ideas.

Introduce the participants to Stage 4: Follow-up: 'Follow-up to marking'.

Now that the participants have an overview of Stage 4 – Follow-up to marking, you are going to show then some prompt statements taken from various educational writer and researchers around the topic of marking and feedback. Each statement can be explored using the think, pair, share approach. This allows participants to really consider the statement themselves first, then build their ideas around what is being said further in a pair before eventually bringing the whole group back together again to gather thoughts and ideas. You could do this by selecting people at random to speak, ask for hands-up feedback or tell a representative from the pair to be ready to feed back to the group on what they talked about.

6. Show and tell (Presentation + reflection + discussion)

(Slide 10)
Take this opportunity to share some ideas with the participants about ways they can best implement follow-up tasks after marking and feedback has taken place by sharing with them a possible strategy that they could use in their classroom tomorrow.

Show and tell

Rework it:

(Do It Again) Give students regular opportunities to respond to your feedback, practise skills they need and gather essential knowledge necessary - Then make them do it again. The same, or a similar task, reworked can really have impact and make sure that

7. The students (Presentation + reflection + discussion)

(Slide 11)
Get participants focusing on the students in their lessons by asking them: Why are we trying to improve the way students approach our marking and feedback?

The students?

This is all about making sure the experience for our students, in our classrooms, is the best experience we are able to give them. So why are we trying to improve our follow up to marking and feedback?

To help our students see the benefit of mastery learning and hard work.

Then have a group discussion about how they see the ideas you've discussed being of benefit to the students if done well. Have an open discussion as a whole group or pair people up first.

This is a nice point to use some pictures of students in your school, examples of students that perhaps would benefit from the improvements that can be made by implementing any of the strategies or ideas to prepare their students for marking and feedback explored today. Make it real for your staff at this point.

8. **Experiential** (Activity + reflection + discussion)

(Slide 12)

This is a chance to help your participants understand the importance of ensuring they are considering the importance of creating a climate of mastery through their follow-up tasks in class. Play the image game with the group.

Experiential

Image game

- One of you has an image. Your job is to give as much high quality feedback as you can to make the other person's representation of it as high quality as possible.
- Firstly, the person who has not seen the image must draw the following thing – a beach at sunset.
- Secondly., you should give them as much detailed feedback as possible to make the image look like yours and they need to draw it again.
- Finally, you must given them feedback again without showing them the image.

You will need to encourage a standard practice of mastery In your classroom as part of the learning and assessing process.

---

9. **Practice and coaching** (Activity + reflection + discussion)

(Slide 13 and 14)

With all the theory that has been covered in today's session your teachers will absolutely want a chance to discuss everything they've learnt. Using a structured coaching method can give them a chance to explore any concerns or questions they may have around the topics covered by this point.

Ask participants to pair up with someone in their group and follow the process of one person talking about an issue or question they have about anything that has been explored today for one minute uninterrupted; then the other person leads them through a GROW coaching discussion (see slide 14). Once one person has

---

Practice

- Pair up in your groups and choose one person to talk for one minute about a problem they are having in relation to today's marking and feedback topic.

- The other person should listen carefully to them.

- Talk to your partner and give them as much detail as possible.

Coaching

- Once they have finished telling you about their problem, take them through the GROW process of coaching to try and see a way forward. Ask them questions to help but do not offer any answers yourself!

- Once you have finished repeat the whole process in opposite roles.

Goal	Reality	Options	Will do / Way forward
What do they want to achieve? Why do they want to achieve it?	Where are they now? What have they already tried?	What are the things that they could try? What have others tried?	What are they going to do now to move forward?

---

gone through this process they should swap roles and complete the activity once again. The issue can be a simple one. Ensure you give teachers enough time to complete the process for both people in the pair.

10. Practice (Activity + reflection + discussion)

(Slide 15)
Once both people in the pair have completed the activity it is a good time to bring the groups back together for a few minutes to share the issues they discussed. Note them down and keep them for future reference and for planning of future sessions. It is right to feed back after this activity but is usually best on a voluntary basis as coaching can be a personal process to go through. Get the teachers discussing how the conversation helped them to solve their problem or if they need more help.

Practice

- What was the result of the discussion in your paired coaching activity?

- Consider how the conversation might help you with your issue as you go forward in your practice.

---

11. Review learning (Reflection + discussion)

(Slide 16)
At the end of the session, ensure that you revisit the session aims and outcomes that you presented at the start and address how each one has gone, acknowledging any that still need to be worked on and any that were achieved particularly successfully.

Reflect and review

Aims

- To explore how to best design effective and impactful follow-up tasks once marking has been returned to students.

- To highlight some key strategies to use.

- To plan how to apply the ideas to your classroom setting.

Individual reflection

- Take a minute to reflect on how you have found this session and what it has made you think about.

Once the aims and outcomes have been discussed give the participants time to reflect personally on the session today and make plans for what they want to do next. This is always better done in silence for a few minutes.

12. Follow-up

(Slide 17)
Before participants leave make sure to wrap up and leave them looking forward to the next session. Remind them of what is required of them to make their training a success by highlighting what they need to commit to do after today's session. Also leave them with a taste of what is to come next time you all meet together and your job here is done! The exciting process of improving their marking and feedback practice has begun.

Follow-up

Commitment to action

- To review the tasks you set following marking and ensure that they are designed to further embed learning and encourage mastery.

Next session

- Explore the manner in which students approach the marking and feedback they receive in your classrooms.

Twilight Session 6: Planning for marking

Planning document

Focus	Notes
Facilitators	• Consider whether you'd like to have any other staff members take a lead of any parts of the training session. • There may very well be some staff who have really come on leaps and bounds during the whole-school focus on marking and feedback in this half term's twilight trainings. Celebrate their achievements by asking them to share their journey to success.
Topics covered	1. Exploration of how to use marking and feedback to inform your planning. 2. Key strategies discussed. 3. Planning for implementation in the classroom.
Preparation tasks	• Organise the training room for how you want the participants to sit and place a list of who is to sit where at the door. • Print key strategies help sheet (slide) for all staff. • Print CPD evaluation document for all staff.
Resources required	• PowerPoint presentation. • Seating plan. • CPD evaluation documents. • Key strategies help sheet. • Examples of marking (staff to bring with them).
Preparation time required	**Beforehand:** • 15 minutes: Email staff and ask them to bring along examples of their marking to the session. • 30 minutes: Familiarisation with and adaption of PowerPoint to suit needs of your particular context. **On the day:** • 15 minutes: Printing off handouts. • 15 minutes: Setting up the room.
Potential problems and solutions	**Problem:** Some participants may feel like they have already completed a full cycle of marking and feedback already: they have prepared the students, done the marking, worked on their student approach to marking and feedback and re-thought follow-up tasks. They may feel this is the end of the process. **Solution:** It is important to remind staff of the importance of marking informing our planning. This session is a very important one designed to help them do this as effectively as possible.
Possible follow-up tasks	Students could be asked to fill in a questionnaire about how they have found the changes that they may have experienced in terms of marking and feedback around the school. An interesting way to gauge the impact the CPD sessions have had on ground level.
Pass it on	A display highlighting the exciting endeavors into improving marking and feedback could be placed up in a prominent area of the school for students, staff and visitors to the school to see.

Detailed session and presentation notes

In this session you will be exploring lots of ideas around how best to use marking and feedback to inform your planning with the teachers in this session.

1. Expectations and ground rules (Discussion + activity)

(Slide 2)
Take the opportunity to set the tone for the session and ensure that everyone is ready to participate actively and positively. There are a list of suggested ground rules provided but do tweak them to suit your school or personal preference.
It is always a good idea to offer the group the opportunity to add any rules they feel are missing. You could ask them to write these up on sticky notes and place them on a wall for the group to view and revisit periodically through the session.

Expectations and ground rules

- Respect the views of others
- Give everyone space to make a contribution
- All questions are valid
- Actively listen
- Take part
- Confidentiality – Chatham House Rules
- Challenge the idea and not the person

Do you have any of your own you would like to add?

---

2. Aims and outcomes – adapted in line with expectations (Presentation)

(Slide 3)
Make sure you take the time to discuss the aims and outcomes in detail and answer any questions or queries that your participants may have regarding the session. This is your chance to tell the story of what is to come in the training; to get them excited, curious and interested in what is to come next. Put the training in context: talk about how the topic relates to your students, your school and the particular teachers in the session.

Aims and outcomes of the session

- To explore how students approach the marking and feedback they receive in your classrooms.
- To highlight some key strategies to use.
- To plan how to apply the ideas to your classroom setting.

---

3. Where are we: Our school (Presentation)

(Slide 4)
Now is your chance to ensure that everyone in the session knows exactly what has already been done, perhaps over the last two years, in your school in terms of using marking to inform planning. Make sure you discuss any projects that have taken place and initiatives that have been rolled out. It is important to be honest and open about what worked well and what was not so successful so that the participants can keep this in mind when they are implementing any changes as a result of today's training. Discuss data and the impact of these initiatives and projects and whether they have been appropriate or useful.

Where are we: Our school

- What do we do well with in terms of our marking and feedback?
- What have we already done to improve our marking and feedback?
- What do we still need to improve?
- What do we want to improve upon next?

4. Where are we: You (Activity)

(Slide 5)

It is important to give all participants time to self-reflect and focus on what they have done already and what they would like to focus on with regards to using

Where we are: You

- What do you feel confidence about in terms of your marking and feedback?
- What have you already done to improve your marking and feedback?
- What do you still need to improve?
- What do you want to improve upon next?

marking to improve planning. You could pause and get participants discussing on their tables at this point. You could then ask for tables to feed back on various discussions they have had in their groups. Alternatively, you could ask participants to silently reflect in a journal or notebook and write about what their future goals are.

5. Theory (Presentation + reflection + discussion)

(Slide 6, 7, and 8)
In this session you will be taking staff through the final step of the five-step marking and feedback cycle outlined.

Introduce the participants to Stage 5: Planning for marking.

Stage 5
Planning for marking

Marking is planning. This is a mantra to live by. The marking and feedback that you undertake should feed directly back into the lesson you are planning for that group. It is all good and well having a termly plan and ploughing through it to ensure that you cover everything you should but have the students really learnt everything that you have diligently taught? If not then what was the point in covering it? Ensuring that they actually get concepts and key knowledge that they need in your lessons is essential for progress with all students. If you are not forming or reworking your planning as you go then you are absolutely going to leave some students behind throughout the term and it is very difficult to get them back once you get to the end of a term or a unit. Ensure that your students work and the marking you conduct informs your planning at regular intervals. (Strategy 8: Student-teacher feedback). Students are telling you what they have gained in your lesson through their work so make sure you are listening!

Now that the participants have an overview of Stage 5 you are going to show them some prompt statements taken from various educational writer and researchers around the topic of marking and feedback. Each statement can be explored using the think, pair, share approach. This allows participants to really consider the statement themselves first, then build their ideas around what is being said further in a pair before eventually bring the whole group back together again to gather thoughts and ideas. You could do this by selecting people at random to speak, ask for hands-up feedback or tell a representative from the pair to be ready to feed back to the group on what they talked about.

Theory

A craftsman is 'someone who has integrity and knowledge, who is dedicated to his work and who is proud of what he does and who he is. Someone who thinks carefully and does things well.' Berger believes that in order to achieve excellence we need to ensure there is a school culture of excellence where an ethic of excellence becomes the norm, excellence is 'born from a culture'.
- Ron Berger

Think: Think about the statement for 30 seconds.

Pair: Pair up with someone in your group and discuss your thoughts.

Share: Be ready to share your ideas.

6. Show and tell (Presentation + reflection + discussion)

(Slide 9)

Take this opportunity to share some ideas with the participants about ways they can best use your marking and feedback to inform your planning by sharing with

Show and tell

Examples of excellence

Every time you are setting students off on a task where by they will be receiving your feedback show them examples of excellence. Examples taken form other students are often the most powerful but you can also look to books and the media.

them a strategy they could use tonight when they are marking and considering their next lesson with the class they are marking work for.

7. The students (Presentation + reflection + discussion)

(Slide 10)
Get participants focusing on the students in their lessons by asking them: Why are we trying to improve our planning using data from our marking? Then have a group discussion about how they see the ideas you've discussed being of benefit to the students if done well. Have an open discussion as a whole group or pair people up first.

This is a nice point to use some pictures of students in your school, examples of students that perhaps would benefit from the improvements that can be made by implementing any of the strategies or ideas to prepare their students for marking and feedback explored today. Make it real for your staff at this point.

The students?

This is all about making the experience for our students, in our classrooms, is the best experience we are able to give them. So why are we trying to improve our planning in the light of our marking?

To get to know out students academically as best we can so we have challenge them as best we can.

---

8. Experiential (Activity + reflection + discussion)

(Slide 11)
This is a chance to help your participants understand the importance of ensuring marking informs your planning of future lessons. Put them into groups to focus on the marking they brought along to the session.

> # Experiential
>
> ## Group planning
>
> - You have been asked to bring along some of your recent marking.
>
> - As a group take each person's marking and help them plan for the next lesson with the marking in mind.
>
>

9. Practice and coaching (Activity + reflection + discussion)

(Slide 12 and 13)

With everything that has been covered in today's session your teachers will absolutely want a chance to discuss everything they've learnt. Using a structured

> # Practice
>
> - Pair up in your groups and choose one person to talk for one minute about a problem they are having in relation to today's marking and feedback topic.
>
> - The other person should listen carefully to them.
>
> - Talk to your partner and give them as much detail as possible.
>
>

Coaching

- Once they have finished telling you about their problem, take them through the GROW process of coaching to try and see a way forward. Ask them questions to help but do not offer any answers yourself!
- Once you have finished repeat the whole process in opposite roles.

Goal	Reality	Options	Will do / Way forward
What do they want to achieve? Why do they want to achieve it?	Where are they now? What have they already tried?	What are the things that they could try? What have others tried?	What are they going to do now to move forward?

coaching method can give them a chance to explore any concerns or questions they may have around the topics covered by this point.

Ask participants to pair up with someone in their group and follow the process of one person talking about an issue or question they have, about anything that has been explored today for one minute uninterrupted; then the other person leads them through a GROW coaching discussion (see slide 12). Once one person has gone through this process they should swap roles and complete the activity once again. The issue can be a simple one. Ensure you give teachers enough time to complete the process for both people in the pair.

10. Practice (Activity + reflection + discussion)

(Slide 14)
Once both people in the pair have completed the activity it is a good time to bring the groups back together for a few minutes to share the issues they discussed. Note them down and keep them for future reference and for planning of future sessions. It is right to feed back after this activity but is usually best on a voluntary basis as coaching can be a personal process to go through. Get the teachers discussing how the conversation helped them to solve their problem or if they need more help.

Practice

What was the result of the discussion in your paired coaching activity?

Consider how the conversation might help you with your issue as you go forward in your practice.

11. Review learning (Reflection + discussion)

(Slide 15)
At the end of the session, ensure that you revisit the session aims and outcomes that you presented at the start and address how each one has gone,

Reflect and review

Aims
- To explore how to use marking and feedback to inform your planning.
- To highlight some key strategies to use.
- To plan how to apply the ideas to your classroom setting

Individual reflection
Take a minute to reflect on how you have found this session and what it has made you think about.

acknowledging any that still need to be worked on and any that were achieved particularly successfully.

Once the aims and outcomes have been discussed give the participants time to reflect personally on the session today and make plans for what they want to do next. This is always better done in silence for a few minutes.

12. Follow-up

(Slide 15)
Before participants leave the session make sure to wrap up and conclude this and the series of sessions. Remind them of what is required of them to make the training a success by highlighting what they need to commit to do following on from today's session and the sessions as a whole.

Follow-up

Commitment to action

- Work on your planning for improvement as a result of your marking of student work.
- Consider the cycle you have been through and what works well for you.
- Tweak the process to suit your needs but make your own marking cycle a conscious process.

Action research: Session 1

Planning document

Focus	Notes
Facilitators	• Consider whether you'd like to have any additional staff members take a lead of any parts of the training session. • There may be staff in your school who have conducted action research before. Ask them to share their experiences and help others be more successful either within the training session or to help you with your planning.
Topics covered	1. Getting to know your group activities. 2. Introduction to action research. 3. Introduction to marking and feedback action research focus areas across the school. 4. Discussion around allocated marking and feedback action research topics. 5. Basic approach to action research explored. 6. Action planning for the project.
Preparation tasks	• Allocate action research topics to particular groups: the groups should be about six–eight people in size and consist of participants from different subject areas or year groups dependent on the type of school you are based in. • Organise the training room to accommodate the action research groups sitting together. • Place a list of the action research groups up at the entrance to the training room. • Print recommended web links list to hand out (also to be emailed after the session). • Print CPD evaluation document for all staff.
Resources required	• PowerPoint presentation. • Seating plan according to research group allocation. • Action plan template. • CPD evaluation documents. • Web links list.
Preparation time required	**Beforehand:** • 30 minutes: Familiarisation with and adaption of PowerPoint presentation to suit needs and teaching context. • 20 minutes: Deciding and setting up the groups staff will be in to conduct action research. **On the day:** • 15 minutes: Printing off handouts. • 15 minutes: Setting up the room.
Potential problems and solutions	**Problem:** Some staff may feel they want to work with members from their department area but have been grouped according to a alternative rationale. **Solution:** Give clear reasoning for the groupings you have chosen; this approach allows every department to have an insight into all subtopics being examined through the marking and feedback action research. Also emphasise that this is a whole-school project so we are all in this together.

Focus	Notes
Possible follow-up tasks	• Group presents results to the whole school at the end of the project. • Group presents results at an evening event for parents.
Pass it on	Details of the action research taking place, the topics covered, updates on progress and then finally the results can be shared on your school website.

Detailed session and presentation notes

In this session you will be introducing participants to action research and their new action research working groups.

1. Expectations and ground rules (Discussion + activity)

(Slide 2)
Take the opportunity to set the tone for the session and ensure that everyone is ready to participate actively and positively. There are a list of suggested ground rules provided but do tweak them to suit your school or personal preference. It is always a good idea to offer the group the opportunity to add any rules they feel

---

Expectations and ground rules

- Respect the views of others
- Give everyone space to make a contribution
- All questions are valid
- Actively listen
- Take part
- Confidentiality – Chatham House Rules
- Challenge the idea and not the person

Do you have any of your own you would like to add?

---

are missing. You could ask them to write these up on sticky notes and place them on a wall for the group to view and revisit periodically through the session.

Be mindful not to skip past this stage or only skim over the ground rules, especially in the first session with a new group. Take the time to explain the reasoning behind the rules without lecturing them. The standard should be high at all times in terms of their participation as well as your delivery so share this with them. You only get the best if you give your best.

2. Aims and outcomes – adapted in line with expectations (Presentation)

(Slide 3)
It is likely that the attendees will have a range of experience and knowledge with regards to action research; some may have taken part in it before and others may never have heard of it. Regardless of whether they have taken part in action research before or not the sessions will be useful to them so it is important to make this clear. Every time you undertake action research in your classroom it is a new experience as you are looking at new students, a new question and new topics. Action research is an ongoing and cyclical process so it is always useful to take part in regardless of prior knowledge and experience.

Aims and outcomes of the session

- To introduce our focus on 'action research'.
- To introduce you to your working group.
- To reveal the action research subtopics.
- To discuss best approaches to the subtopics.
- To examine examples of action research.
- To begin to form an action plan.

Outline why action research is being undertaken in your school setting. Reasons may include:

- it is a way to improve whole-school policies based on what you find out in your classroom, rather than just results from any school
- it puts the students at the centre of your teaching and learning improvements.

Make sure you take the time to discuss the aims and outcomes in detail and answer any questions or queries that your participants may have regarding the session. This is your chance to tell the story of what is to come in the training; to get them excited, curious and interested in what is to come next. Put the training in context: talk about how the topic relates to your students, your school and the particular teachers in the session.

3. Where are we: Our school (Presentation)

(Slide 4)
Now is your chance to ensure that everyone in the session is familiar with the Action research projects that have been undertaken in your school recently and how successful they were. It is important to be honest and open about what worked well and what was not so successful so that the participants can keep this in mind and learn from the mistakes whilst undertaking their action research project. Discuss data and the impact of the projects.

Where are we: Our school

- What do we do well with in terms of our marking and feedback?
- What have we already done to improve our marking and feedback?
- What do we still need to improve?
- What do we want to improve upon next?

---

4. **Where are we: You** (Activity)

(Slide 5)

It is important to give all participants time to self-reflect and focus on any action research they have taken part in, or on the areas of their marking and feedback they want to improve by taking part in this action research project. You could pause and get participants discussing on their tables at this point. You could then ask for tables to feed back on various discussions they have had in their groups. Alternatively, you could ask participants to silently reflect in a journal or notebook and write about what their future goals are.

Where we are : You

- What areas of your marking and feedback practice do you feel confident about?
- What have you already done to improve your marking and feedback?
- What do you feel you still need to improve?
- What do you want to improve upon next?

---

5. **Theory** (Presentation + reflection + discussion)

(Slide 6, 7 and 8)

All participants will now be clear that marking and feedback is the key focus and will be thinking about their own practice as well as what has gone on around the school in recent history. They now need to be introduced to the concept of action research, even if they have done it before. There are different ways of undertaking action research so it is important that they are clear about what your process will be. You need to give clear guidelines and have open discussions on what is right for your school setting, your students and your topic of marking and feedback.

Now is a good time to tell attendees that the action research topics have already been chosen for them and allocated to specific cross phase/subject groups so that all phases/subjects get an insight into all topics being researched.

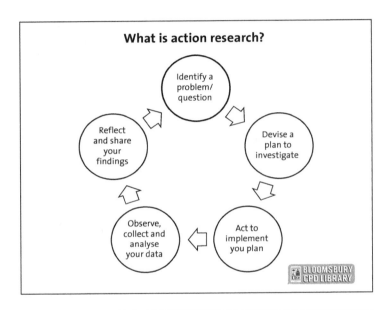

To help shape your discussions and allow participants to fully understand action research and begin to think about what it might look like in their classrooms, show them the action research video and explore the action research cycle diagram below.

Action research overview video shown –
https://www.youtube.com/watch?v=ZhiZdh85R3w

Once the approach of action research has been introduced, show participants some prompt statements taken from various educational writers on the topic of action research. Each statement can be explored using the think, pair, share approach. This allows participants to really consider the statement themselves first, then build their ideas around what is being said further in a pair before eventually bringing the whole group back together again to gather thoughts and ideas. You could do this by selecting people at random to speak, ask for hands-up feedback or tell a representative from the pair to be ready to feed back to the group on what they talked about.

The aim of this activity is to bring to their attention the studies and thinking that is out there about the action research process not to dictate to them how they should approach their own action research. The process of academic discussion around action research should encourage participants to think a little more deeply about the process they are about to undertake.

Theory

> The systematic recording of what actually happens in working circumstances can be a powerful political tool. The same can be said of studies of the 'mismatch' between what is textbook pedagogic 'good practice' and what actually happens. (George and Cowan, 1997; George, 2001.)

Think: Think about the statement for 30 seconds.

Pair: Pair up with someone in your group and discuss your thoughts.

Share: Be ready to share your ideas.

---

6. Case study (Presentation + reflection + discussion)

(Slide 9)
Discuss some basic principles of action research at this point such as:

- Be mindful not to change things before the action research is undertaken; as far as possible, try to observe life in the classroom as it normally really is.
- Look at the data that you collect in detail and from many different angles over a sustained period of time as you may well find that more detail becomes apparent as time moves forward.
- When you write up your explanations keep them grounded firmly in the data you have collected.

To get participants to see what action research might look like in a real classroom, take them through a case study of the full action research process, shown in the flow chart below:

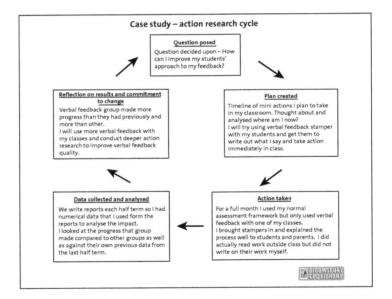

7. The students (Presentation + reflection + discussion)

(Slide 10)
You need to refocus your participants on the students in their classroom after all the talk about action research theory and remind them of the reason we try to get better at what we do every day.

Begin by asking the group how they see any of the theories or ideas in practice being of benefit to the students if done well. Have an open discussion as a whole group or pair people up first; make the decision on how to structure the discussion based on how well the group has shared or reflected in the different parts of the training session so far.

This is a nice point to use some pictures of students in your school, examples of students that perhaps would benefit from the improvements that can be made by implementing any of the ideas or theories explored today. Make it as real for your staff as possible.

The students?

This is all about making sure the experience for our students in our classrooms, is the best experience we are able to give them. So why are we undertaking this action research?

- To get to know our students learning even better
- To improve our classroom practice

---

8. Experiential (Activity + reflection + discussion)

(Slide 11)

Now you need to encourage members in the different groups to get to know each other a bit better before they're given their action research topic. The game of 'Life highlights' is designed to allow the groups to get to know the other members a little bit better professionally as well as keeping the mood positive and upbeat by looking at professional highlights.

Experiential

Life highlights – Instructions:

- Close your eyes for one minute and consider the best moments of your teaching life.
- Your search for highlights is about to be narrowed. Take a moment to decide what 30 seconds of your teaching life you would want to relive if you only had thirty seconds left in your life.
- Now go around the group and discuss your personal teaching-life highlights.

You are about to work in this group for some time so it is really good to get to know them professionally a little better.

---

9. Action research topics (Presentation)

(Slide 12)

Now that the groups have started to get to know one another professionally and the topic of action research has been looked at in some detail, it is time to reveal the topics that each group have been given.

Action research groups

- Group 1 – Does **verbal feedback** have a positive impact on student progress?
- Group 2 – Does the use of **codes** have a positive impact in student progress?
- Group 3 – **Does the use of** digital marking tools have a positive impact on student progress?
- Group 4 – Does the use of **feedback task lessons** directly after every piece of marked work have a positive impact on student progress?
- Group 5 – Does the use of **peer marking** have a positive impact on student progress?
- Group 6 – Does the **elimination of grades** have a positive impact on student progress?

---

10. **Practice and coaching** (Activity + reflection + discussion)

(Slides 13 and 14)
Once the topics have been revealed, the participants will most definitely want to
talk about their area of research so provide them with a structured way of doing

---

Practice

Exploring issues with your topic:

- Pair up in your groups and choose one person to
  talk for one minute about a problem you have had
  in the past related to the action research topic you
  have been allocated.
- The other person should listen carefully to them.
- Talk to your partner and give them as much detail as
  possible.

Coaching

- Once they have finished telling you about their problem, take them
  through the GROW process of coaching to try and see a way forward.
  Ask them questions to help but do not offer any answers yourself!

- Once you have finished repeat the whole process in opposite roles.

Goal	**Reality**	**Options**	**Will do /** **Way forward**
What do they want to achieve? Why do they want to achieve it?	Where are they now? What have they already tried?	What are the things that they could try? What have others tried?	What are they going to do now to move forward?

---

it. Using a structured coaching method can give them a chance to explore any concerns or questions they may have around the topics covered so far.

Ask participants to pair up with someone in their group and follow the process of one person talking about an issue or question they have about anything that has been explored today for one minute uninterrupted; then the other person leads them through a GROW coaching discussion (see slide 12). Once one person has gone through this process they should swap roles and complete the activity once again. The issue can be a simple one. Ensure you give teachers enough time to complete the process for both people in the pair.

11. Practice (Activity + reflection + discussion)

(Slide 15)
Once both people in the pair have completed the activity it is a good time to bring the groups back together for a few minutes to share the issues they discussed. Note them down and keep them for future reference and for planning of future sessions. It is right to feed back after this activity but is usually best on a voluntary basis as coaching can be a personal process to go through. Get the teachers discussing how the conversation helped them to solve their problem or if they need more help.

Practice

Exploring issues with your topic:

- Share the discussion from the paired coaching activity about your action research topic with the rest of your group.
- What issues and ideas for ways forward have you come up with as a group? Note them down on the large paper on your tables.

---

12. **Action research planning template** (Activity + discussion)

(Slide 16)

The final activity in the session is to show the participants the action research planning template and give them time to begin plotting out ideas of things they might like to do to start the action research process. Hand out copies of the action research template with the recommended websites printed on the back. These can be found on the last two (hidden) slides of the PowerPoint for today's session.

Either give the groups time to help one another plan their research in the session, or organise a meeting separate from today's session where the groups come together and help one another action plan once they have had time to think about their topics and how they may approach it in their classrooms.

Action research planning

Action research topic: Does **verbal feedback** have a positive impact on student progress?

Action/steps	Person(s) responsible	Timeframe start/end	Resources needed	Evaluation
Use verbal feedback with one class	Bob	Day 1 and for the duration	Class lists Timetable Verbal feedback stamps	Data from class analysed and compared to prior data and other similar class's data

13. **Review learning** (Reflection + discussion)

(Slide 17)

At the end of the session, ensure that you revisit the session aims and outcomes that you presented at the start and address how each one has gone, acknowledging any that still need to be worked on and any that were achieved particularly successfully.

Reflect and review

Aims and outcomes

- To introduce our focus on 'action research'.
- To introduce you to your working group.
- To reveal the action research subtopics.
- To discuss best approaches to the subtopics.
- To examine examples of action research.
- To begin to form an action plan.

Individual reflection

Take one minute to reflect on how you have found this session and what it has made you think about.

Once the aims and outcomes have been discussed give the participants time to reflect personally on the session today and make plans for what they want to do next. This is always better done in silence for a few minutes.

14. Follow-up

(Slide 18)

Before participants leave the session make sure to wrap up and conclude this and the series of sessions. Remind them of what is required of them to make the training a success by highlighting what they need to commit to do following on from today's session and the sessions as a whole.

Follow-up

Commitment to action:

- Continue the action plan you have started to form today
- Choose the students you intend to include
- Gather the resources and inform necessary parties
- Work with your group to help one another

Next session:

- We will be reviewing the groups and individuals progress
- Providing you with further advice and guidance

Action research: Session 2

Planning document

Focus	Notes
Facilitators	• Consider whether you'd like to have any other staff members take a lead of any parts of your training session. • There may be members of staff in your school who have conducted action research before. Ask them to share their experiences and help others be more successful. • Some staff may be really excelling in their action research projects. If this is the case then get them to lead a section of this training session to inspire others.
Topics covered	1. Group working analysis activity. 2. Intermediate approach to action research explored. 3. Review of progress in action research projects. 4. Action planning review for the project.
Preparation tasks	• Ask all groups to give you a brief update on where they are in their action research projects prior to the session so you know how to pitch this training session. • Organise the training room to accommodate the action research groups sitting together. • Print CPD evaluation documents for all staff.
Resources required	• PowerPoint presentation. • Seating plan. • 'Making action research work' slide printed for all staff. • CPD evaluation documents.
Preparation time required	**Beforehand:** • 30 minutes: Familiarisation with and adaption of PowerPoint presentation to suit your needs and teaching context. • 60 minutes: Collating progress feedback from each action research group and adapting focus as necessary. **On the day:** • 15 minutes: Printing off handouts. • 15 minutes: Setting up the room.
Potential problems and solutions	**Problem:** Some groups may be having issues with working together or seeing links across departments with the focus topic. **Solution:** The 'Making action research work' slide provides top tips on how to make groups work efficiently and see links regardless of age group or subject specialism.
Possible follow-up tasks	• Action plans revised. • Group presents results to the whole school at the end of the project. • Group presents results at an evening event for parents.
Pass it on	Get each group to write a blog post for the school blog about their individual findings and what they thought about the process of action research, providing tips for other teachers.

Detailed session and presentation notes

This is your second session with the action-researching teachers so they are on their way with their projects but will be at different points and taking many different approaches due to the variety of topics being looked at across the school.

1. Expectations and ground rules (Discussion + activity)

(Slide 2)
Take the opportunity to set the tone for the session and ensure that everyone is ready to participate actively and positively. There are a list of suggested ground rules provided but do tweak them to suit your school or personal preference. It is always a good idea to offer the group the opportunity to add any rules they feel are missing. You could ask them to write these up on sticky notes and place them on a wall for the group to view and revisit periodically through the session.

Expectations and ground rules

- Respect the views of others
- Give everyone space to make a contribution
- All questions are valid
- Actively listen
- Take part
- Confidentiality – Chatham House Rules
- Challenge the idea and not the person

Do you have any of your own you would like to add?

---

2. Aims and outcomes – adapted in line with expectations (Presentation)

(Slide 3)
At this point groups will all be at different stages in the action research journey. Some may be finding the process really positive and others struggling more. Be

prepared to be open and positive towards all experiences. This session is aimed at catching up with all the groups and troubleshooting any issues they are experiencing as well as highlighting any excellent practice going on around the school.

Make sure you take the time to discuss the aims and outcomes in detail and answer any questions or queries that your participants may have regarding the session. This is your chance to tell the story of what is to come in the training; to get them excited, curious and interested in what is to come next. Put the training in context: talk about how the topic relates to your students, your school and the particular teachers in the session.

Aims and outcomes of the session

- To reflect on how our groups are working.
- To explore our focus of action research.
- To analyse our groups' research progress.
- To plan for the rest of the action research.

---

3. Where are we: Our school (Presentation)

(Slide 4)

It is a good idea to check in with the groups periodically in person and via email throughout the research to see where they are with their planning and implementation of the action research projects. You can check who needs more assistance and who is excelling in their projects. You should also have the head of department report back on how their teams are finding focusing on different topics within their subject area. This gives you a slightly different perspective of the general picture around the school. With this knowledge in mind give an update overview to the entire group. You can choose to name people as you update or keep it anonymous and talk more generally.

Where are we: Our school

- What are do we doing well in our projects so far?
- What have we already done to improve our marking and feedback?
- What do we still need to improve?
- What do we want to improve upon next?

---

4. Where are we: You (Activity)

(Slide 5)

It is important to give all participants time to self-reflect and focus on what they have done already and what they would like to focus on in their marking and

---

Where are we: You

- What do areas of your project do you feel confident about?
- What have you already done to improve your marking and feedback?
- What do you still need to improve?
- What do you want to improve upon next?

---

feedback action research before you carry on with the training. You could pause and have a discussion on tables at this point. You could then ask for tables to feed back on various discussions they have had in their groups. Alternatively, you could ask participants to silently reflect in a journal or notebook and write about what they envision as the next steps for the projects.

5. Theory (Presentation + reflection + discussion)

(Slides 6, 7 and 8)
To help shape your discussions and allow participants to further consider the action research process, display the action research process diagram and discuss the ongoing nature of action research. You can explore the fact that one action research question can lead to another and another and so on...

Once the alternative action research approach diagram has been discussed you are going to show participants some prompt statements taken from various educational writer and researchers around the topic of action research. Each statement can be explored using the think, pair, share approach. This allows participants to really consider the statement themselves first, then build their ideas around what is being said further in a pair before eventually bringing the whole group back together again to gather thoughts and ideas. You could do this by selecting people at random to speak, ask for hands-up feedback or tell a representative from the pair to be ready to feed back to the group on what they talked about.

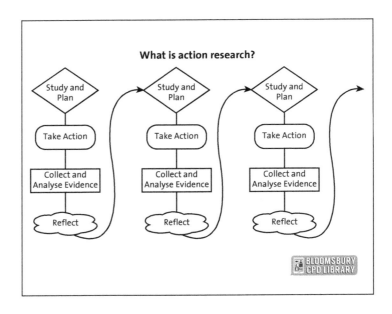

This activity is just to bring their attention to the studies and thinking what is out there on the action research process not to dictate participants on how they should approach their own action research. The process of academic discussion around action research should just make participants think a little more deeply about the process they are currently undertaking.

Theory

As Bentz and Shapiro (1998) state: 'Action research is less a separate culture of inquiry than it is a statement of intention and values. The intention is to change a system, and the values are those of participation, self-determination, empowerment through knowledge, and change.'

Think: Think about the statement for 30 seconds.

Pair: Pair up with someone in your group and discuss your thoughts.

Share: Be ready to share your ideas.

Theory

Some people place more emphasis on the 'research' element. As Kemmis and McTaggart say (op cit), it should be more 'systematic' than teaching. Stenhouse (1985) suggests that action research 'should be characterized by systematic self-enquiry' (p8, our emphasis) and should contribute to 'a theory of education and teaching which is accessible to all teachers.' (1975, cited in Cohen and Manion, 1989, p.217.)

Think: Think about the statement for 30 seconds.

Pair: Pair up with someone in your group and discuss your thoughts.

Share: Be ready to share your ideas.

6. Show and tell (Presentation + reflection + discussion)

(Slide 9)

Take this opportunity to share some ideas with the participants about the kind of things they could be including as a part of their action research projects. As you will have an understanding of where the groups are from your enquiries prior to the CPD event today you could point out any groups that have chosen to incorporate these approaches into their action research projects to bring the ideas to life.

End this section of the session by opening up the discussion to any other approaches that groups have used in their action research so far by posing the question: Are there any other ways you have thought of or have read about being using?

Show and tell – Approaches to action research

- Photos
- Audio files
- Videos
- Field notes
- Interaction analysis
- Interviews
- Questionnaires
- Ratings scales
- Diaries / Logs
- Observations
- Data analysis

Are there any other ways you have thought or, read about of being using?

BLOOMSBURY CPD LIBRARY

---

7. The students (Presentation + reflection + discussion)

(Slide 10)

You need to refocus your participants on their students after all the talk about the progress of their action research projects and to remind them of the reason we try to get better at what we do every day.

The students?

This is all about making sure the experience for our students, in our classrooms, is the best experience we are able to give them. So why are we doing this Action research?

- To become masters of our trade
- To get them better results

Begin by asking the group how they see what they have undertaken already as being of benefit to the students they teach. Have an open discussion as a whole group or pair people up first; make the decision on how to structure the discussion based on how well the group has shared or reflected in the different parts of the training session so far.

This is a nice point to use some pictures of students in your school, examples of students that perhaps would benefit from the improvements that can be made by implementing any of the ideas or theories explored today. Make it as real for your staff as possible.

8. Experiential (Activity + reflection + discussion)

(Slide 11)

This is a chance for your groups to work through any issues they may be having with their action research projects. It will help them to see another side of any problems they're having and will also help them to bond with their team once again meaning that they will be more willing to help one another outside of the CPD sessions even though they are in different departments. Get them taking part in the winner/loser activity.

Experiential

Winner / Loser Activity - Instructions:

Negative – Person 1 tell person 2 about something negative that has happened during your action research. You must continue to talk for two minutes about your story and give as much detail as you can.

Positive – Person 1 tells the same story but this time relates only good things that came from the experience. Person 2 must help them explore the good that came from the bad.

9. **Practice and coaching** (Activity + reflection + discussion)

(Slide 12, 13 and 14)
Now that the groups have started on their action research projects, planned out a possible way through the project and discussed a possible issue in the last task it is time for the GROW coaching to begin again. They can use the same issue they explored in the last activity or they can mix it up and use another one or one they foresee as a possible problem as the project nears its close.

Remind them of what everyone is doing across the school and get them really thinking about what they want to do better before the action research project ends.

Ask participants to pair up with someone in their group and follow the process of one person talking about an issue or question they have about anything that has been explored today for one minute uninterrupted; then the other person leads them through a GROW coaching discussion (see slide 14). Once one person has gone through this process they should swap roles and complete the activity once again. The issue can be a simple one. Ensure you give teachers enough time to complete the process for both people in the pair.

Action research groups

- Group 1 – Does **Verbal Feedback** have a positive impact on student progress?
- Group 2 – Does the use of **codes** have a positive impact in student progress?
- Group 3 – **Does the use of** digital marking tools have a positive impact in student progress?
- Group 4 – Does the use of **feedback task lessons** directly after every piece of marked work have a positive impact in student progress?
- Group 5 – Does the use of **peer marking** have a positive impact in student progress?
- Group 6 – Does the **elimination of grades** have a positive impact in student progress?

Practice

Exploring issues with your topic:

- Pair up in your groups and choose one person to talk for one minute about a problem you have had in the past related to the action research topic you have been allocated.
- The other person should listen carefully to them.
- Talk to your partner and give them as much detail as possible.

Coaching

- Once they have finished telling you about their problem, take them through the GROW process of coaching to try and see a way forward. Ask them questions to help but do not offer any answers yourself!

- Once you have finished repeat the whole process in opposite roles.

Goal	**Reality**	**Options**	**Will do / Way forward**
What do they want to achieve? Why do they want to achieve it?	Where are they now? What have they already tried?	What are the things that they could try? What have others tried?	What are they going to do now to move forward?

10. Practice (Activity + reflection + discussion)

(Slide 15)

Once both people in the pair have completed the activity it is a good time to bring the groups back together for a few minutes to share the issues they

Practice

Exploring issues with your topic:

- As a group you should share your discussion from the paired coaching activity around your action research topic.
- What issues and ideas for ways forward have you come up with as a group? Note them down on the large paper on your tables.

discussed. Note them down and keep them for future reference and for planning of future sessions. It is right to feed back after this activity but is usually best on a voluntary basis as coaching can be a personal process to go through. Get the teachers discussing how the conversation helped them to solve their problem or if they need more help.

11. Review learning (Reflection + discussion)

(Slide 16)

At the end of the session, ensure that you revisit the session aims and outcomes that you presented at the start and address how each one has gone, acknowledging any that still need to be worked on and any that were achieved particularly successfully.

Once the aims and outcomes have been discussed give the participants time to reflect personally on the session today and make plans for what they want to do next. This is always better done in silence for a few minutes.

Reflect and review

Aims

- To reflect on how our groups are working.
- To explore our focus of action research.
- To analyse our groups research progress.
- To plan for the rest of the action research.

Individual reflection

Take minute to reflect on how you have found this session and what it has made you think about.

---

12. Follow-up

(Slide 17)

Before participants leave the session make sure to wrap up and conclude this and the series of sessions. Remind them of what is required of them to make the training a success by highlighting what they need to commit to do following on from today's session and the sessions as a whole.

Follow-up

Commitment to action:

- Revise your action plan.
- Start to plan how and when you will gather and anlayse data.
- Work with your group to help one another.

Next session:

- We will be reviewing the groups and individuals progress.
- Providing you with further advice and guidance.
- Preparing for your final presentations.

Action research: Session 3

Planning document

Focus	Notes
Facilitators	• Consider if you'd like to have any other staff members take a lead of any part of the training session. • There may be members of staff in your school who have conducted action research before so use them to share their experiences and help others be more successful. • Some staff may be much further ahead than others and may already have some data to share. If this is the case then get them to lead a section of the session to inspire others.
Topics covered	1. Group presentations activity. 2. Advanced approach to action research explored. 3. Review of progress in action research projects. 4. Action planning review for the project. 5. Planning for the final presentations.
Preparation tasks	• Ask all groups to give you a brief update on where they are in their action research project prior to the session so you know how to pitch this training session. • Organise the training room to accommodate the action research groups sitting together. • Print CPD evaluation documents for all staff.
Resources required	• PowerPoint presentation. • Seating plan. • 'Presenting action research' slide printed for all staff. • CPD evaluation documents.
Preparation time required	**Beforehand:** • 30 minutes: Familiarisation with and adaption of PowerPoint presentation to suit your needs and teaching context. • 60 minutes: Collating progress feedback from each action research group and adapting focus as necessary. **On the day:** • 15 minutes: Printing off handouts. • 15 minutes: Setting up the room.
Potential problems and solutions	**Problems:** Some groups may be anxious about presenting their findings to an audience. **Solution:** The 'Presenting action research' slide provides top tips on how to present action research projects successfully.
Possible follow-up tasks	• Action plans revised. • Group presents results to the whole school at the end of the project. • Group presents results at an evening event for parents.
Pass it on	Film the presentations of final results and share them on your school YouTube channel. (You should set up a YouTube channel for your school if you don't have one!)

This is your final session with the action-researching teachers before the final presentation event. It is at this point that you want to decide what format you want the presentations to take. You could have all staff seated in the main hall or meeting space to listen to groups presenting their findings via PowerPoint. You could consider having a more visual relaxed presentation event and invite groups to put together display boards with images, write ups and data outlining the process they have been through and their findings. If you go for the latter you could have the display boards set up around the hall and have staff walk around discussing as they go. You could even invite parents and other interested external parties in to view them. This really helps to promote the great stuff that is going on around the school.

Groups are deep into their projects but will be at different points and taking many different approaches due to the variety of topics being looked at across the school.

1. **Expectations and ground rules** (Discussion + activity)

(Slide 2)
Take the opportunity to set the tone for the session and ensure that everyone is ready to participate actively and positively. There are a list of suggested ground rules provided but do tweak them to suit your school or personal preference.

Expectations and ground rules

- Respect the views of others
- Give everyone space to make a contribution
- All questions are valid
- Actively listen
- Take part
- Confidentiality – Chatham House Rules
- Challenge the idea and not the person

Do you have any of your own you would like to add?

It is always a good idea to offer the group the opportunity to add any rules they feel are missing. You could ask them to write these up on sticky notes and place them on a wall for the group to view and revisit periodically through the session.

2. Aims and outcomes – adapted in line with expectations (Presentation)

(Slide 3)
At this point groups will all be at different stages in the action research journey. Some may be finding the process really positive and others struggling more. Be prepared to be open and positive towards all experiences. This session is aimed at catching up with all the groups and troubleshooting any issues they are experiencing as well as highlighting any excellent practice going on around the school.

Make sure you take the time to discuss the aims and outcomes in detail and answer any questions or queries that your participants may have regarding the session. This is your chance to tell the story of what is to come in the training; to get them excited, curious and interested in what is to come next. Put the training in context: talk about how the topic relates to your students, your school and the particular teachers in the session.

Aims and outcomes of the session

- To reflect on how our groups are working.
- To deeply consider focus of action research.
- To analyse our groups' research progress.
- To plan for the group presentations.
- To plan for the rest of the action research.

3. **Where are we: Our school** (Presentation)

(Slide 4)

It is a good idea to check in with the groups periodically in person and via email throughout the research to see where they are with their planning and implementation of the action research projects. You can check who needs more assistance and who is excelling in their projects. With everyone's feedback and your observations of the work you have seen so far in mind give an update overview to the entire group. You can choose to name people as you update or keep it anonymous and talk more generally.

Where are we: Our school

- What are do we doing well in our projects so far?
- What have we already done to improve our marking and feedback?
- What do we still need to improve?
- What do we want to improve upon next?

---

4. **Where are we: You – self-evaluation** (Activity)

(Slide 5)

It is important to give all participants time to self-reflect and focus on what they have done already and what they would like to focus on in their marking and feedback action research before you carry on with the training. You could pause and have a discussion on tables at this point. You could then ask for tables to feed back on various discussions they have had in their groups. Alternatively, you could ask participants to silently reflect in a journal or notebook and write about what they envision for the final steps of their project and future goals.

Where are we : You

- What do areas of your project do you feel confident about?
- What have you already done to improve your marking and feedback?
- What do you still need to improve?
- What do you want to improve upon next?

BLOOMSBURY
CPD LIBRARY

5. Theory (Presentation + reflection + discussion)

(Slide 6)

It is time to show participants some prompt statements one last time taken from various educational writers and researchers around the topic of action research.

Theory

McNiff (1988) suggests that action research should encourage: '...teachers to develop theories and rationales for their practice and to give reasoned justification for their public claims to professional knowledge...it is this systematic enquiry made public which distinguishes the activity as research.'

Think: Think about the statement for 30 seconds.

Pair: Pair up with someone in your group and discuss your thoughts.

Share: Be ready to share your ideas.

BLOOMSBURY
CPD LIBRARY

Each statement can be explored using the think, pair, share approach. This allows participants to really consider the statement themselves first, then build their ideas around what is being said further in a pair before eventually bringing the whole group back together again to gather thoughts and ideas. You could do this by selecting people at random to speak, ask for hands-up feedback or tell a representative from the pair to be ready to feed back to the group on what they talked about.

This activity is just to bring to their attention the studies and thinking that is out there about the action research process not to dictate to them how they should approach the final steps of their own action research. The process of academic discussion around action research should just make participants think a little more deeply about the process they are currently undertaking.

6. Show and tell (Presentation + reflection + discussion)

(Slide 7)
Take this opportunity to share some ideas with the participants about the things they may want to keep in mind as they start to plan for their final presentations of the action research projects. The participants are all focusing on very different topics so one person's data may look very different to another person's data and that is OK. The important aspect of the action research is for the participants to investigate a question or problem in marking and feedback in their classroom with their students and then take actions and make changes with this now information in mind.

Show and tell – presenting your findings

Focus questions	Ideas
What did you do?	Action planning Working with others Resources used Action taken Problems experienced Highlights
What did you discover?	What were your results? How do they compare to prior results of similar groups results? Was there anything surprising?
What did you, or will you change as a result of your enquiry?	What are your actions points from the enquiry? What are you going to look at next?

7. The students (Presentation + reflection + discussion)

(Slide 8)
You need to refocus your participants on their students after all the talk about the progress of their action research projects and and remind them of the reason we try to get better at what we do every day.

Begin by asking the group how they see what they have undertaken already as being of benefit to the students they teach. Have an open discussion as a whole group or pair people up first; make the decision on how to structure the discussion based on how well the group has shared or reflected in the different parts of the training session so far.

This is a nice point to use some pictures of students in your school, examples of students that perhaps would benefit from the improvements that can be made by implementing any of the ideas or theories explored today. Make it as real for your staff as possible.

The students?

This is all about making the experience for our students, in our classrooms, is the best experience we are able to give them.

So why are we doing this action research?

- To understand what works in our classrooms
- To give our students better chances in life

---

8. Experiential (Activity + reflection + discussion)

(Slide 9)
This is a chance for your groups to begin to consider how they will best present their finding to others. The game of 'Articulate' will be a little bit of fun but also

---

Experiential

Articulate – Instructions

- One person - pick up the card in the centre of the table.

- You must try to get your team to guess what the word is without saying the word, drawing anything of making any actions or gestures.

- Everyone in your team must have a go at explaining the item written on the cards.

You will need to articulate your points well in your presentations so get practicing in using your words to help others understand what is in your mind.

---

will get them to consider how they can use their language best to really get people to understand them and what process they have been through over the course of the action research project.

9. Practice and coaching (Activity + reflection + discussion)

(Slides 10 and 11)
Now that the groups have been working on their action research projects for some time and can see the end-game in sight it is time for the GROW coaching to begin again. They can use the same issue they explored in the last activity or they can mix it up and use another one or one they foresee as a possible problem as the project nears its close.

Ask participants to pair up with someone in their group and follow the process of one person talking about an issue or question they have, about anything that has been explored today for one minute uninterrupted; then the other person leads them through a GROW coaching discussion (see slide 11). Once one person has gone through this process they should swap roles and complete the activity once again. The issue can be a simple one. Ensure you give teachers enough time to complete the process for both people in the pair.

Practice

Exploring issues with your topic:

- Pair up in your groups and choose one person to talk for one minute about a possible problem you are dealing with or can foresee within the data collection and analysis or presentation process
- The other person should listen carefully to them.
- Talk to your partner and give them as much detail as possible.

Coaching

- Once they have finished telling you about their problem, take them through the GROW process of coaching to try and see away forward. Ask them questions to help but do not offer any answers yourself!

- Once you have finished repeat the whole process in opposite roles.

Goal	Reality	Options	Will do/ Way forward
What do they want to achieve? Why do they want to achieve it?	Where are they now? What have they already tried?	What are the things that they could try? What have others tried?	What are they going to do now to move forward?

10. **Practice** (Activity + reflection + discussion)

(Slide 12)

Once both people in the pair have completed the activity it is a good time to bring the groups back together for a few minutes to share the issues they discussed. Note them down and keep them for future reference and for planning of future sessions. It is right to feed back after this activity but is usually best on a voluntary basis as coaching can be a personal process to go through. Get the teachers discussing how the conversation helped them to solve their problem or if they need more help.

The final activity in the session is to allow the participants time to show one another their action research plans and discuss how they are going. They could also discuss how they would like to present their findings to other staff members and possibly parents and carers if that is what the school has decided.

You can give the groups a longer period of time to help one another plan or you could organise a meeting separate from today's session over the course of the next week to allow for the discussions to continue.

Practice

Exploring issues with your topic:

- As a group you should share your discussion from the paired coaching activity around your action research topic.
- What issues and ideas for ways forward have you come up with as a group? Note them down on the large paper on your tables.

---

11. Review learning (Reflection + discussion)

(Slide 13)
At the end of the session, ensure that you revisit the session aims and outcomes that you presented at the start and address how each one has gone, acknowledging any that still need to be worked on and any that were achieved particularly successfully.

Once the aims and outcomes have been discussed give the participants time to reflect personally on the session today and make plans for what they want to do next. This is always better done in silence for a few minutes.

Reflect and review

Aims

- To reflect on how our groups are working.
- To deeply consider focus of action research.
- To analyse our groups research progress.
- To plan for the group presentations.
- To plan for the rest of the action research.

Individual reflection

>   Take minute to reflect on how you have found this session and what it has made you think about.

---

12. Follow-up

Before participants leave the session make sure to wrap up and conclude this and the series of sessions. Leave them with a feeling of excitement about the wrapping up of their action research projects. They should be looking towards the presentations next time you all meet together. Leave them excited about what the results of the action research may be and what those findings might mean for their classroom practice, the school and the students.

Follow-up

Commitment to action:
- Complete any last tasks in your action plan
- Gather and anlayse the data
- Work with your group to help one another
- Decide how you will present your findings

Next session:
- We will be presenting our final write up and findings form the action research project.
- We will be planning for future possible enquiries.

Bibliography and further reading

Berger, R. (2003), *An Ethic of Excellence: Building a Culture of Craftsmanship with Students. Heinemann*

Berger, R. *'Doing good work' – the Ron Berger interview'* (www.youtube.com/watch?v=THfL7SYRcDU)

Berger, R. *'Cultivating an ethic of excellence'* (vimeo.com/21983525)

Bjork, R. *'Desirable difficulties perspective on learning'* (http://bjorklab.psych.ucla.edu/RABjorkPublications.php)

Bjork, R. *'Bjork Learning and Forgetting Lab Publications'* (http://bjorklab.psych.ucla.edu/RABjorkPublications.php)

Clarke, S. (2014), *Outstanding Formative Assessment: Culture and Practice. Hodder Education*

Dweck, C. (2007), *Mindset: The New Psychology of Success: How We Can Learn to Fulfil our Potential. Ballantine*

Hattie, J. (2012), *Visible Learning for Teachers: Maximising Impact on Learners. Routledge*

Hattie, J. (2012), *Feedback in schools* (Chapter 8) in Sutton, R. M., Hornsey, M. J. and Douglas, K. M. *Feedback: The Communication of Praise, Criticism and Advice.* Peter Lang

Hattie, J. *'Feedback in schools'* (http://visible-learning.org/2013/10/john-hattie-article-about-feedback-in-schools)

Lemov, D. (2010), *Teach Like a Champion: 49 Techniques That Put Students on the Path to College.* Jossey-Bass

Bibliography and further reading

Lemov, D., Woolway, E. and Yezzi, K. (2012), *Practice Perfect: 42 Rules for Getting Better at Getting Better*. Jossey-Bass

Morrison-McGill, R. (2013), *100 Ideas for Secondary Teachers: Outstanding Lessons*. Bloomsbury

Rosenthal, R. and Jacobson, L. (1992), *Pygmalion in the Classroom: Teacher Expectation and Pupils' Intellectual Development* (revised edn). new edition 2003 Crown House Publishing

Rosenthal, R. *'The pygmalion effect and the power of positive expectations'* (www.youtube.com/watch?v=hTghEXKNj7g)

Smith, J. (2010), *The Lazy Teacher's Handbook: How Your Students Learn More When You Teach Less*. Crown House Publishing

Wiliam, D. and Black, P. (1990) *Inside the Black Box: Raising Standards Through Classroom Assessment*. GL Assessment

Wiliam, D. 'Feedback on learning' (www.journeytoexcellence.org.uk/resourcesandcpd/biographies/biogdylanwiliam.asp)

Wiliam, D. 'Self- and peer-assessment' (www.journeytoexcellence.org.uk/resourcesandcpd/biographies/biogdylanwiliam.asp)
Willingham, D. T. (2009), *Why Don't Students Like School? A Cognitive Scientist Answers Questions About How The Mind Works and What It Means For The Classroom*. Jossey-Bass